AMERICAN SCIENCE FICTION AND FANTASY WRITERS

Collective Biographies

AMERICAN SCIENCE FICTION AND FANTASY WRITERS

Claire L. Datnow

MEDIA CENTER
MEADE MIDDLE SCHOOL
1103 26th STREET
FT. MEADE, MARYLAND 20755

Enslow Publishers, Inc.

44 Fadem Road   PO Box 38
Box 699   Aldershot
Springfield, NJ 07081   Hants GU12 6BP
USA   UK

http://www.enslow.com

Library of Congress Cataloging-in-Publication Data

Datnow, Claire L.
   American science fiction and fantasy writers / by Claire L. Datnow.
      p.   cm. — (Collective biographies)
   Contents: Robert A. Heinlein — Isaac Asimov — Frederik
Pohl — Ray Bradbury — Frank Herbert — Poul Anderson —
Andre Norton — Madeleine L'Engle — Ursula K. Le Guin —
Octavia E. Butler.
   Includes bibliographical references and index.
   ISBN 0-7660-1090-2
   1. Authors, American—20th century—Biography—Juvenile
literature.   2. Fantastic fiction—Authorship—Juvenile literature.
3. Science fiction—Authorship—Juvenile literature.   [1. Authors,
American.   2. Science fiction—History and criticism.
3. Fantasy—History and criticism.]   I. Title. II. Series.
PS129.D36   1999
813'.08760905—dc21   98-8846
                                                   CIP
                                                   AC

Printed in the United States of America

10 9 8 7 6 5 4 3 2 1

To Our Readers:
All Internet addresses in this book were active and appropriate when we went to press.
Any comments or suggestions can be sent by e-mail to Comments@enslow.com or to
the address on the back cover.

Illustration Credits: Photo by Jay Kay Klein, pp. 14, 21, 24, 31, 34, 41, 44,
50, 54, 61, 64, 70, 74, 79, 82, 91, 104, 109; Photograph by Marian Wood
Kolisch, pp. 94, 100.

Cover Illustration: Photo by Jay Kay Klein

Contents

Introduction

The works of the ten American authors discussed in this book reflect the changes that took place in science fiction and fantasy writing during the twentieth century. These authors helped to introduce and to shape those changes. Starting as action-packed adventures published in cheap magazines of the 1920s, science fiction evolved into the more thought-provoking novels published today.

There is no firmly agreed-upon definition of science fiction or fantasy. However, science fiction is nearly always set in the future and usually includes imagined discoveries and inventions that could be explained by science.[1] When science fiction includes ideas that cannot be explained by science, then it is labeled fantasy. In simple terms then, science fiction deals with what could happen and could be explained whereas fantasy deals with what could not. But there is often no clear line between the two because many writers blend ideas from science fiction and fantasy.

For example, most people would agree that Ursula K. Le Guin's Earthsea books are science fiction because in them she attempts to explain events and to describe the worlds she creates in realistic details. Yet Earthsea is a fantasy world where magic works and talking dragons exist. In contrast, stories by Ray Bradbury and Andre Norton are more fantasy than science fiction because their outlook is mystical or even antiscientific. In Ray Bradbury's *Illustrated Man*, for example, the tattoos on a man's skin come to life.[2]

Scholars believe that the English author Mary Wollstonecraft Shelley's *Frankenstein*, published in 1818, was the first genuine science fiction novel. *Frankenstein* explores the relationship between mankind and science. The central character, Victor Frankenstein, is a student of chemistry. After years of study, he unlocks the secrets of life. He collects human remains and brings to life a creature that is almost a devil. After Victor abandons his creature, it stalks him all over Europe. *Frankenstein* became the model for science fiction for the next forty years.

Jules Verne, a Frenchman, made the next contribution to science fiction. In *Twenty Thousand Leagues Under the Sea*, Verne's protagonist, Captain Nemo, is a scientist. The action takes place aboard the *Nautilus*, a highly advanced submarine. Verne's novel reflected society's growing interest in science and technology.

H. G. Wells, a British writer, is another important founder of science fiction. *The Time Machine* (1895) and *The War of the Worlds* (1898) warned of future disasters, alien invasions, and cosmic catastrophes. *The Island of Dr. Moreau* (1896) introduced the problems of mutation and genetic engineering. Wells and Verne developed two science fiction themes still popular today: space adventures and voyages to unknown places on earth.

At the start of the twentieth century, American writers like L. Frank Baum and Edgar Rice Burroughs brought science fiction to the attention of an even wider audience. Baum's Marvelous Land of Oz series (1900) and Burroughs's Tarzan of the Apes series (1912) were extremely popular. Burroughs, unlike the aforementioned writers, had an interest in romantic but unrealistic (nonscientific) adventures, which helped to create what later became known as fantasy fiction.

Around this time many new, inexpensive magazines appeared, which helped writers such as Burroughs to establish their reputations. Then in 1926, Hugo Gernsback published the first true science fiction magazine, *Amazing Stories*. The earliest issues of Gernsback's magazine printed Verne, Wells, and other well-known authors. Gernsback also published new writers such as E. E. "Doc" Smith, who would influence the next generation of science fiction writers, including Robert Heinlein, Isaac Asimov, Frederik Pohl, and Poul Anderson.

Gernsback published what became known as space operas in his pulp magazines. (They were known as pulps because they were printed on cheap wood-pulp paper that quickly turned yellow.) These were action-packed adventures centered on muscular heroes who rescued sweet space maidens from wicked villains and destroyed alien worlds with space machines. They also featured eye-catching, colorful art. Some critics called space opera nothing but cheap and poorly written entertainment. Though much space opera was not well written, some stories showed creativity and skill.

John W. Campbell, Jr., became editor of *Astounding Science Fiction* (originally *Astounding Stories*) in 1937. Campbell founded what became known as the golden age of science fiction pulp magazines, which lasted from about 1938 to 1945. He was a great teacher and shaped the writing careers of many, including Robert Heinlein, Isaac Asimov, and Frederik Pohl. During this time the rules for science fiction were laid out.

Campbell believed that science fiction was a form of literature that explored the ways in which technology and science changed human society for the better (but sometimes for the worse). He insisted that his writers be scientifically accurate and that they write about what was probable, not impossible. They had to base their work on hard sciences, such as physics, chemistry, geology, and astronomy. Under the guidance of Campbell, writers continued to use ideas from space operas but with higher standards of writing, more complex plots, and more fully developed characters.

After World War II, pulp magazines began to lose their popularity and a new trend started. Collections of the best science fiction stories, first published in magazines during the golden age, began to appear in book form. Frederik Pohl promoted this change by selling up-and-coming science fiction writers directly to well-known book publishers. Pulp magazines had helped to establish the reputations of many authors. However, after the 1950s book publishing boom, pulp writers were viewed as second-rate authors.

Around 1947 Robert Heinlein made a breakthrough by becoming the first American science fiction author published in general magazines rather than in pulp magazines. Ray Bradbury also sold many of his early stories to general magazines, which helped to promote the popularity and acceptance of science fiction and fantasy.

Other changes took place in the late 1960s and early 1970s, a period known as the new wave of science fiction. Under the influence of the new wave, writers began to break the rules established by Campbell. They gave new life to science fiction by drawing ideas from soft sciences—anthropology, sociology, psychology—rather than hard sciences only. As a result, their tales became more thought-provoking. Authors explored social problems such as drugs, overpopulation, and environmental destruction. Frederik Pohl later said, "The thing that the 'new wave' did that I treasure was to shake up old dinosaurs, like Isaac [Asimov], and for that matter me . . . and show them that you do not really have to construct a story according to the 1930s pulp or Hollywood standards."[3]

The increasing number of women writers since the late 1960s also transformed science fiction. Authors such as Andre Norton, Madeleine L'Engle, and Octavia Butler created a host of smart and strong female characters. These protagonists are very different from the weak female characters first portrayed in pulp science fiction. These authors also explored issues of sexism and racism. Their stories impressed upon readers the need to be open-minded about those different from themselves.

After you have read the biographies of the ten science fiction writers in this book, you may want to read some of the wonderful tales they wrote. Perhaps those stories will inspire you to write your own original stories.

Robert A. Heinlein

Shaking the Reader Loose

Robert Anson Heinlein once said, "I write stories for money. What I wanted to be was an admiral."[1] Heinlein always felt disappointed that illness cut short his career in the United States Navy. But he became one of the most brilliant American science fiction writers of the twentieth century.

Robert was born July 7, 1907, on a farm in the small town of Butler, Missouri. Soon after, the Heinlein family moved to Kansas City. Robert spent the summers in Butler with his grandfather Lyle, a doctor. He remembered going with him on his rounds in a horse-drawn buggy. Many years later, in his novel *Time Enough for Love* (1973), Heinlein wrote about a horse-and-buggy doctor, based on his grandfather.[2] Heinlein felt that he had been strongly

Robert A. Heinlein

"influenced by [his] parents [Rex, an accountant, and Bam, his mother] and six siblings and everything I have seen, touched, eaten, endured, heard, and read."[3] But what really sparked his imagination as a boy were exciting science fiction adventure stories.

In high school, Robert was a superior student. After graduating in 1924, he wanted to follow his older brother's example and become an officer in the Navy. "I worked two years writing letters and applications and finally got the appointment," he said.[4] Heinlein did well at the United States Naval Academy in Annapolis, graduating twentieth in his class of 243.

He served on the *Lexington,* one of the world's first modern aircraft carriers. On the *Roper* he served as a gunnery officer. But Heinlein's bright naval career came to a sudden end. Ill with tuberculosis, he was forced to retire in 1934. Yet he never stopped thinking of himself as a naval officer. Later he used these experiences to write believable stories, with carefully thought-out technical details, about strong men of action.[5]

This was a very difficult time for Heinlein. He had married Leslyn MacDonald, and at twenty-seven he had to find a new career. Jobs were hard to find because America was going through the economic downturn known as the Great Depression. For the next five years Heinlein tried one thing after another without much luck. He wanted to do graduate work in physics and mathematics at the University of

California, Los Angeles. But his health was still poor, so he moved to Colorado to recover. Heinlein then sold real estate and operated a Colorado silver mine. He later ran for the California State Assembly but came in second. At age thirty-two, he was still without a job and found himself broke. The need for money pushed him into his writing career.[6]

In 1939, he saw an advertisement in *Thrilling Wonder Stories* offering a fifty-dollar prize for the best amateur fiction. Quickly he wrote his first short story, "Life-Line." But he did not send it in because he found out that *Astounding Science Fiction* was paying a penny a word. Since his story ran to seven thousand words, he sent it to John Campbell, editor of *Astounding Science Fiction.* Campbell bought it for twenty dollars more than Heinlein would have won in the contest. Thus began Heinlein's career as a writer.

Between 1939 and 1942, most of Heinlein's stories became part of his Future History series. On a road trip from New York to California, in a new 1939 Chevy, Heinlein had a brilliant idea—a wall chart that would outline the future. In May 1941, *Astounding Science Fiction* printed Heinlein's chart, which showed where his previous stories belonged and where new stories would fit.

By 1942, when he quit writing to return to the Navy, Heinlein had published three novels and about thirty stories that made up a future history. Readers of *Astounding Science Fiction* eagerly looked forward to each new story in the saga. The Future History chart distinguished Heinlein as one of the most ambitious and inventive writers of modern science fiction. Since then, other science fiction writers have copied Heinlein's idea and created future histories of their own.

During World War II, Heinlein went to work as an engineer in the Naval Air Experimental Station at Philadelphia, where he tested materials used in flight. There he met Virginia Gerstenfeld, a test engineer and chemist. He married Virginia in 1948, after having divorced his first wife, Leslyn, in 1947.[7]

When World War II ended, Heinlein began writing again, but he did not continue his Future History series. He wrote instead about the glory of space travel. His stories were published in the *Saturday Evening Post*, the first science fiction ever to be published in a magazine other than the pulps.

Then, beginning with *Rocket Ship Galileo* (1947), Heinlein wrote a series of space novels for young adults. In this first novel, Ross, Art, and Morrie are teenagers who take a trip to the moon in an atomic-powered rocket. In 1950, *Rocket Ship Galileo* became the basis for a science fiction movie, *Destination Moon*. Heinlein also used his experiences at Annapolis to write *Space Cadet* (1948), which became the basis for the television serial *Tom Corbett: Space Cadet*.

For the next twelve years, Heinlein continued to write for young adults—one book a year for the

Christmas market.[8] In many of these stories—*Space Cadet, Farmer in the Sky* (1950), *Starman Jones* (1953), and *Tunnel in the Sky* (1955)—he expertly develops the theme of the rite of passage, the struggle to grow from childhood to adulthood. His novels were considered to be the best American science fiction up to that time.[9] Among them, *Double Star* (1956), about an unsuccessful actor who pretends to be a politician, won a Hugo Award. (Named for Hugo Gernsback, the Science Fiction Achievement Award is presented annually by the World Science Fiction Society [WSFS].)

Heinlein had decided to make money at writing science fiction, and he had succeeded in doing it.

Though Heinlein liked to tell John Campbell that he wrote only for the money, it was not true. His stories, especially those written in the 1940s and 1950s for teenagers, are full of his hopes and dreams. Around him Heinlein saw a greedy and dangerous society. Through science fiction, he found a way to warn ordinary folk about dishonest people and to imagine inhabiting a better future.

In the 1960s, Heinlein's writing became less optimistic and less concerned with new technology, and it began to include more fantasy. He became more concerned with expressing his opinions on political and social problems. *Starship Troopers* (1959) is a violent tale of interstellar war. In it, Heinlein tries to persuade readers that his young hero's change, from a man of peace to a professional soldier, is good.

During this period Heinlein wrote his classic work of science fiction, *Stranger in a Strange Land* (1961). It became his best-known work and won a 1962 Hugo Award. The novel sold over 2 million copies and made many fans. It also shocked many of his readers because of its extreme views. In *Stranger in a Strange Land* Heinlein seemed to advocate unlimited freedom in love and in political action.

Stranger in a Strange Land is the story of Valentine Michael Smith. Raised on Mars by Martians, Smith is brought back to Earth as an adult. Smith is able to control objects and even his bodily functions with the power of his mind. Slowly, Smith begins to understand, or "grok," human beings. Eventually he starts a new religion, the Church of All Worlds. As the messiah of this religion, Smith teaches his disciples three ceremonies: water-sharing, grokking, and communal sex.

Cults sprang up around *Stranger in a Strange Land*, and Heinlein was considered to be a spiritual guru. His followers even went so far as to start a real-life Church of All Worlds. They bothered him so much that he had to build a fence around his home to keep them out. Heinlein was amazed by their behavior. He had *not* been trying to give his readers answers to religious questions but had been trying to get them to think for themselves.[10]

Heinlein's writing during the 1970s reflected the violent and frightening times. America was losing a bloody war in Vietnam. On college campuses, anti-war demonstrations resulted in battles between students and police. Martin Luther King, Jr., the leader of the civil rights movement for African Americans, was assassinated in 1968. The assassination of Robert Kennedy shocked the world in June 1968. In Heinlein's *I Will Fear No Evil* (1970), Johann Sebastian Smith, a very old and dying man whose brain is transplanted into the body of his young female secretary, says: "Back in the old days . . . the United States was a fine country, brimming with hope. But today the best thing most young people can do is stay at home. . . . It's better than dropping out or turning on to drugs."

This theme of survival may have been on Heinlein's mind because he had been near death at least three times. In 1934, he had tuberculosis, in 1970 he underwent major surgery, and in 1977 he had a bypass for a blocked artery to his brain.

Time Enough for Love, or the Lives of Lazarus Long (1973) introduced the immortal Lazarus Long. Long reappears as the central character in several other books published during the 1980s. Heinlein uses Long to put forward his own views. These novels were criticized for their lack of action and for their preachy style.[11]

At the time of his death in 1988, Heinlein had won four Hugo Awards and the first Grand Master

Heinlein was honored with the first ever Grand Master Award, for lifetime achievement.

Award. Forty million copies of his books have been printed in thirty different languages. He is considered by many to be the father of modern science fiction.[12] He led the way in creating believable characters and vivid settings that were different from the old science fiction tales, which were filled with long, sometimes boring explanations.

By building on actual scientific research being done in the nation's laboratories, he made science fiction more believable than it had been. He said, "I regard myself as a professional prophet—a man who makes an honest attempt to evaluate the probabilities."[13] Indeed, when men walked on the moon in 1969, Heinlein's earlier tales about the conquest of space seemed to be coming true. He predicted the coming of the atomic bomb and nuclear power plants. For example, in 1940 he wrote "Blowups Happen," a tale about the psychological stress of those working in nuclear power plants. "Solution Unsatisfactory" (1941) weaves a story about using radioactive dust as a weapon of war.

Heinlein put forward ideas that attracted but also angered and even shocked some of his readers. "I was trying to shake the reader loose from [old ideas] and induce him to think for himself, along new and fresh lines," he said.[14]

Isaac Asimov

Astonishing, Astounding, and Amazing

Isaac Asimov's career has been compared to the science fiction magazines he wrote for: astounding, astonishing, and amazing. From humble beginnings as a poor immigrant, he rose to become one of the most influential writers in America.

Judah and Anna Rachel Berman Asimov immigrated from Petrovichi, Russia, to the United States in 1923, when Isaac was just three years old. Isaac celebrated January 2, 1920, as his birth date, but he did not have the actual record of his birth. By 1926 his father had saved enough money to buy a candy store in Brooklyn. The store was open seven days a week and eighteen hours a day, so Isaac had to pitch in too.[1] Every day after school young Isaac worked in the family store.

Isaac Asimov

Isaac was never bored, because he could read the stories in the pulp magazines that were sold in the store. At first, his father would not allow him to read such "trash," but Isaac convinced him that *Science Wonder Stories* was all about science.[2] He read the magazines as soon as they came in, because his father did not allow him to keep unsold copies.[3] His father got him a library card, and Isaac remembered coming home with three books from the library, one tucked under each arm and reading the third.[4] Thus, from an early age Isaac was hooked on science fiction.

As a young science fiction fan, he began writing letters to magazines, commenting on the stories he had read. Soon he was submitting his own stories to John Campbell, the editor of *Astounding Science Fiction*. Isaac took the bus down to Campbell's office to deliver his first story. Although his story was rejected, he was able to meet the editor in person. Asimov wrote, "I couldn't believe it when the receptionist told me that Mr. Campbell would see me. What made it possible was that I was not . . . unknown to him. He had been receiving and printing my letters, so he knew I was a serious science fiction fan."[5] From then on Campbell gave Isaac advice and encouragement and later began to publish his stories.

Isaac attended Boys High School in Brooklyn when he was twelve years old. This school accepted only the brightest students. Isaac was shocked to find that he was not the smartest student, as he had been in previous schools. Despite this, he graduated in 1935 at age fifteen. All along he continued writing and submitting stories.

At nineteen, Asimov joined a science fiction fan club called the Futurians.[6] Until then, he had been too busy working in the candy store to make friends. While some of the kids at school disliked him for being a know-it-all, the Futurians enjoyed Asimov's lively conversation.[7] They became his lifelong friends. Many of them went on to become famous writers, among them Frederik Pohl and Robert Heinlein. In fact, Pohl published Asimov's early stories in *Astonishing Stories* and *Super Science Stories.*

On graduation from high school, Isaac applied to Columbia University but failed to get in.[8] Instead, he received a full scholarship to attend Seth Low Junior College, then part of Columbia University. He obtained his undergraduate degree in chemistry from Columbia in 1939.

Though his father wanted him to go to medical school, he was not accepted. Instead, he entered graduate school at Columbia to study chemistry. Although he felt disappointed, he knew that he was not cut out to be a doctor. While in graduate school, he continued to write and publish stories. He completed his M.A. degree in 1941.

At twenty-two, Asimov met Gertrude Blugerman on a blind date. He fell in love with her and talked her into marrying him. Gertrude always believed that he would succeed as a writer.[9]

World War II halted his studies. During the war he worked at the Naval Air Experimental Station in Philadelphia with fellow writer Robert Heinlein. Then the army drafted him and shipped his unit out to Hawaii, but he never saw any fighting.

On his return, he went back to graduate school, and he completed a Ph.D. in chemistry in 1948. Asimov applied for jobs at several universities without any luck. Then in 1949, Professor William C. Boyd, who had read and admired Asimov's stories, hired him as an associate professor of biochemistry at the Boston University School of Medicine (BUSM).[10]

Just a few weeks after he accepted the job, he sold his first full-length novel, *Pebble in the Sky.* The novel appeared in print in 1950 and became one of four future history novels he would write. The sale of his first novel tempted Asimov to become a full-time writer. But he decided to play it safe, and he went to work at Boston University.

Part of his work there involved doing research, but he lacked skill at lab work and so avoided it. This made him unpopular with the other professors, who expected him to be part of their research teams. On the bright side, he loved teaching the medical students and did it so well that they applauded him during lectures.[11] Asimov's "wise-guy personality" also may have made him unpopular with some of his coworkers.[12] He admitted that he could be hard to get along with and did not always try to please those in charge. As a result, his enemies at BUSM succeeded in firing him in 1958. Many years later, when Asimov became famous, the university invited him back as an honored guest.

After leaving BUSM, Asimov tried without success to find work as a chemist. While working at the university he had continued to write and to publish stories and novels.[13] Asimov realized that he was now earning more than enough from his writing to support his wife, Gertrude, and two children, David and Robyn, and did not need another job.

As early as 1941 he had begun writing what were to become his most famous works: "Nightfall," the Robot series, and the Foundation series. "Nightfall" (1941) earned him a place as a major writer of science fiction. The original idea came from Campbell. "Nightfall" tells the story of a planet that has never experienced darkness because it has six suns. The inhabitants are overcome by panic when there is a total eclipse of the six suns and darkness falls for the first time. It is not the darkness that makes them go mad but the thousands of glittering stars that become visible to them for the first time. Many consider "Nightfall" his best story and even the best science fiction story of all time.

During the time he was working on "Nightfall," he also worked on the Robot series. Asimov's stories about robots were collected in *I, Robot* (1950). The robot stories are scientific detective tales in which robots develop problems that have to be solved by scientists. The third tale, "Liar!" introduces Asimov's three laws of robotics. A robot may not harm humans, it must obey orders, and it should protect itself from harm. These laws influenced many other science fiction writers. Most science fiction writers at the time described robots as frightening metal monsters. Asimov believed that robots could help mankind:

> There was a time when humanity faced the universe alone and without a friend. Now he has the creatures to help him: stronger creatures than himself, more faithful, more useful, and absolutely devoted to him. Mankind is no longer alone.
>
> —Asimov, *I, Robot*

The Foundation series proved even more popular than the Robot series. Unlike the robot stories, which take place on Earth in the near future, the Foundation trilogy tells of a vast Galactic Empire thousands of years in the future. In this series, Hari Seldon, the last great scientist of the first empire, starts a Foundation on the planet Terminus. The Foundation's purpose is to put together a galactic encyclopedia. However, Seldon has to prevent the takeover of Terminus and the Foundation by evil invaders. Seldon devises a plan. He uses the science of "psychohistory" to predict and control the future. His plan is upset by the Mule, who uses paranormal powers in ways Seldon is unable to predict.

Under the name Paul French, Asimov wrote the Lucky Starr series, his first fiction for young readers. These are space operas about Lucky Starr, a space ranger who outwits space pirates, poisoners, mad scientists, and interstellar spies.

After "Nightfall" and the Robot, Foundation, and Lucky Starr series, Asimov wrote almost no science fiction. Between 1958 and 1980 he turned his energy to writing nonfiction. During this period Asimov wrote hundreds of books on science, history, humor, and literature. He had a special talent for explaining difficult ideas simply. He wanted to help educate Americans, and he earned the nickname the Great Explainer.

Beginning in November 1958, he wrote a column for *The Magazine of Fantasy and Science Fiction.* His column won a Hugo Award for "adding science to science fiction."[14] In 1976, he started *Isaac Asimov's Science Fiction Magazine,* the first new science fiction magazine in the United States since 1955. "Every month his face could be seen, with its bushy white muttonchops [sideburns], on the cover. . . . Often he'd be costumed as an astronaut [to remind] us that it's not the jocks but the brains who [shape the future]."[15]

From the volume of his work, it is clear that Asimov loved writing. He admitted that he spent so much time writing that he had little time to spend with his family. After thirty years of marriage, Asimov divorced Gertrude in 1972. Soon after he

A science fiction fan himself, Asimov soon found himself signing autographs for his own fans.

married Janet Jeppson, a psychiatrist and writer whom he had met at a science fiction convention. Issac and Janet collaborated on several books; they began a robot series for children, the Norby books.

Asimov kept on writing to the very end of his life. He died in 1992 at the age of seventy-two. Though honored with the Hugo, Nebula (awarded annually by the Science Fiction and Fantasy Writers of America [SFFWA]), and Grand Master awards, and many honorary degrees, he remained a homebody. He liked nothing better than writing away in his Manhattan apartment. Asimov felt that he had lived a good life and had reached his goals as a writer. He published over five hundred books. "I felt Heaven to be the act of writing, and I have been in Heaven for over half a century," he said.[16]

Frederik Pohl

Master of Buying, Selling, and Writing Science Fiction

Frederik Pohl was born November 26, 1919, in New York City, the son of Fred George Pohl and Anna Jane (Mason) Pohl. Though he was not very interested in school, he loved to read. The summers spent on his uncle's farm in Harlem, Pennsylvania, passed by pleasantly for young Frederik because he had plenty of time to read.

On the farm he had fun swimming in the brook, hunting in the woods, or teasing the neighbor's bull, but he did not like farm chores. To avoid work, he found the perfect place to hide, the farmhouse attic. Though it reeked of tobacco and the sour smell of heat, there Frederik could read to his heart's content. Years later he remembered, "The truly marvelous thing was that in a corner of the attic was a

Frederik Pohl

treasure-trove of old pulp magazines, hundreds of them."[1] From age ten to age twelve, he read every scrap of science fiction he knew to exist. "My head was popping with spaceships and winged girls and cloaks of invisibility, and I had no one to share it with," he said.[2]

The carefree years of the 1920s came to an end with the Great Depression of the 1930s. Frederik's family, like many others, had to struggle to survive. There were homeless and jobless people everywhere. To get these people back to work, great changes had to be made in government and society. These hard times made a lasting impression on Frederik. The stories he later wrote reflected the need to make constant change a force for the betterment of society.

As a fourteen year old at Brooklyn Technical High School, Frederik joined one of the first science fiction clubs ever organized. He became the editor of the club's fan magazine. According to Frederik, when professional writers came to their meetings, the fans felt that they "sat at the feet of the masters . . . and resolved to be just like them."[3] He was hooked for life.

He and his friends founded other science fiction clubs in the New York area, including the famous Futurians. Editing and publishing their magazines, or fanzines, was a good learning experience for Pohl. While still in high school, he started submitting his writing to *Astounding Stories* and *Science Wonder Stories*, using pen names such as James MacCreigh and Warren F. Howard. With all these activities his grades fell, and Frederik decided to drop out of school. Thus he began his long and varied career in science fiction. He became a master at buying, selling, and writing science fiction.

As a seventeen-year-old high school dropout, he tried to pass himself off as a literary agent, selling his own stories and those of his friends from the fan clubs. If a magazine published a story he submitted, he made a small profit.

As a young literary agent, he got to meet John Campbell, the editor of *Astounding Science Fiction*. Pohl was impressed by Campbell's ideas, and he learned much about the writing and selling of science fiction from him. Pohl remembered walking through the printing plant past great strong-scented rolls of pulp paper to get to Campbell's office. A large sharp-featured man, Campbell looked like a bear with glasses. He would swivel around in his chair, then toss out a suggestion for a story or discuss the problems of science fiction with him. Pohl said, "Every word he said I memorized. . . . I had never known anyone else who knew about these things."[4]

Despite his efforts, Pohl's agency made very little money. Now nineteen, Pohl began to shop around for a job.[5] He was hired by Campbell as editor of two new pulp magazines, *Astonishing Stories* and *Super Science Stories*, and he worked there from 1941 to 1943. At this time he married Doris Baumgardt, but the marriage lasted only a few years. While working as editor of these magazines, Pohl published some of his own stories. At that time, writers only got paid one penny per word, so they wrote quickly and without revision. As a result, many of the stories were badly written. Pohl, the whiz-kid editor, had to correct and rework them.

World War II halted his writing for a time. Pohl served in the United States Air Force, 12th Weather Squadron, from 1943 to 1945. He was assigned the job of writing and editing the squadron's newspaper. Meanwhile, he had divorced Doris Baumgardt and fallen in love with Dorothy LesTina. He found a way to get special leave to go to Paris and marry Dorothy.

After the war, he started another literary agency. When Doubleday, a well-known publishing company, decided to publish science fiction books, Pohl's talent as a salesman came into play. Until then, science fiction had never appeared in hardcover. Pohl made a success of selling up-and-coming writers such as Isaac Asimov to Doubleday.

Pohl also worked as a copywriter and editor with Popular Science publishers. In 1948, he resigned to become a full-time literary agent. His marriage to Dorothy LesTina was not going well, and they divorced. In 1949, he married Judith Merril, a science fiction writer. This third marriage also ended in divorce in 1952. Soon after, Pohl decided to write full-time. "I spend some time writing every day of my life, even when I don't feel like it—even when I have a good excuse not to," Pohl says.[6]

While working as a literary agent, Pohl began writing a novel with Cyril Kornbluth, whom he had met at the Futurians Club. For a time, Pohl had worked with an advertising agency that paid him a good salary. The advertising world later sparked ideas for many tales, such as "The Midas Plague" (1954). "The Midas Plague" is a tall tale about wealthy sellers and poor people. The poor are forced to consume huge amounts of food churned out by automated factories. To solve this problem, robots are created to consume the food. Together with Kornbluth, Pohl promoted the new trend that was just developing in science fiction—social criticism. These stories are comic satires. Satires help us to think more clearly about social problems by magnifying and laughing at them.

Their first story came out in serial form under the title "Gravy Planet" (published in *Galaxy* in 1952). It was later published in paperback as *The Space Merchants* (1953). In this story, Pohl and Kornbluth criticized everything they hated about advertising. It is told in the first person by Mitchell Courtenay, an advertising manager who plots to take over Venus. The overpopulated Earth needs Venus's resources to survive. After Mitch experiences the hard life of a worker, he becomes a consie. As a consie he turns his talents toward conserving the world that he once looted. Pohl and Kornbluth tell a gripping tale of a world almost destroyed by greed. *The*

Space Merchants is both funny and frightening. It has become a classic and has never been out of print.

By his own count in the 1950s, Pohl had published about forty short stories, a dozen or so science fiction novels, and eight books. He also collaborated with his fourth wife, Carol Metcalf Ulf, whom he married in 1952. Together they edited several anthologies (collections of stories). The many social and political changes of the 1960s inspired Pohl, like other science fiction writers, to continue writing satires that pointed out the errors of big government, big business, and the military.

While working as an assistant editor at *Galaxy* magazine and *If* from 1961 to 1969, he published some of the best science fiction writers of the time. At Ace and Bantam books, Pohl created a growing market for hardcover science fiction. His Star Science Fiction series led the way with original anthologies.

In the 1970s, when Pohl quit editing science fiction magazines and returned to writing full-time, his writing improved greatly. In *Man Plus* (1976) and *Gateway* (1977), he skillfully combined humor with serious themes. Pohl warned his readers that the earth could be destroyed by overpopulation, a new wave theme. In *Man Plus*, astronaut Roger Torraway becomes a cyborg, half man, half machine, capable of living on Mars. The hero of *Gateway*, Robinette Broadhead, survives contact with a black hole that trapped nine others. The story tells what Broadhead found on Gateway and why he is so unhappy despite his riches. *Gateway* was the first of the Heechee Saga series, which follows humanity's exploration of the galaxy, using artifacts left behind by aliens. Included in the Heechee series are *Beyond the Blue Event Horizon* (1980), *Heechee Rendezvous* (1984), and *The Annals of the Heechee* (1987).

All along, even though he had dropped out of high school, Pohl continued to educate himself on many subjects. Pohl said, "I don't think of myself as a scholar . . . [but] I love learning, especially history, politics, and above all science."[7] He put this self-taught knowledge to such good use that he became a well-known writer and radio and television personality. He was also in demand as a public speaker. He lectured around the world, and he enjoyed exploring new places and meeting new people.[8] Pohl states that although he never attended college, and, in fact, left high school without graduating, "that was a long time ago, in a different world. I would not recommend following my example."[9]

Pohl's fifth and present wife is Elizabeth Anne Hull, whom he married in 1984. Dr. Hull is a college professor and a leading member of the Science Fiction Research Association. Besides writing, Pohl remains active in public life. In 1996, Pohl assisted his wife in her (unsuccessful) run for the United States Congress.[10]

For his achievements he has been honored with many awards. Among them are the Hugo Awards in

Pohl holds one of the many awards he has won during his lifetime.

1966, 1967, and 1968 for "Best Editor." *Man Plus* received the 1977 Nebula. *Gateway* won the John W. Campbell Award (from the WSFS) in 1978, the Nebula in 1978, the Hugo in 1978, and the Prix Apollo in 1979. In 1980, he won the first and only American Book Award given in the category of science fiction.

Critics have said that Pohl's tales are corny, not very believable space adventures. However, as a tireless editor, agent, and writer since his teens, Pohl has made a great contribution to the development of science fiction writing. Over the years his style, which skillfully mixes the comic and satiric, has become more complex, his characters more thoughtful, and his plots and settings more realistic. Pohl himself agrees that science fiction should be more than fast-moving entertainment, it should aim to meet high standards. Indeed, he goes so far as to say that science fiction is significant because it is the only kind of writing that deals with the most important fact of life today: change.[11]

Ray Bradbury

Dreaming the Past-Future

When the circus came to the small town of Waukegan, Illinois, young Ray Bradbury fell completely under the spell of Mr. Electrico, the magician who performed with the circus.

> Mr. Electrico sat in his electric chair, being fired with ten billion volts of pure blue sizzling power. . . . He brushed an Excalibur sword over the heads of the children, knighting them with fire. When he came . . . to me, he tapped me on both shoulders and then the tip of my nose. The lightning jumped into me. Mr. Electrico cried "Live forever!"[1]

From that moment, the art of magic set Ray's imagination on fire. Soon after, he began writing

Ray Bradbury

fantasy stories. Indeed, magic is a recurring theme in much of his adult writing.

Ray Douglas Bradbury was born on August 22, 1920, to Leonard Spaulding and Esther (Moberg) Bradbury. Ray's mother read the Brothers Grimm and L. Frank Baum to him. He remembered the first film she took him to see, the horror classic *The Hunchback of Notre Dame*.[2] His Aunt Neva, a theatrical costume designer, made him masks and puppets and told him the stories of Edgar Allan Poe.

Later, Ray collected then-popular Buck Rogers comic strips and read *Amazing Stories* magazine. In the public library, he found the adventure stories of Edgar Rice Burroughs, Tom Swift, Jules Verne, and H. G. Wells. He said, "[I knew] that the library was to be my college, my university."[3] Today, Bradbury urges young people to seek knowledge from every source: Read books in print or on CD-ROM, audio tapes, or films, which are books in different shapes. Listen to music. Go to art galleries. And keep on writing.

In 1932, during the Depression, his father lost his job as a telephone lineman. He took the family to Tucson, Arizona, to look for work. The family moved to Los Angeles in 1934 when Ray was fourteen years old. Ray loved the city from the start and has lived there ever since. However, his childhood memories of midwestern small-town life have always remained clear in his mind and have reappeared in his stories.

Unlike his athletic brother Skip, Ray was a dreamer bullied by his peers.[4] Though he recalled his high school years as unhappy ones, he found outlets in art, drama, and journalism. His high school English teacher, Jennet Johnson, encouraged him to write and became his lifelong friend.

In his free time, Ray tried to see every motion picture released. Living in Hollywood, he collected autographs of his favorite stars. He even found the nerve to introduce himself to the hit comic team of George Burns and Gracie Allen. As a result he was hired to write comic skits for the *Burns and Allen* radio show.[5]

In 1937, he discovered the Los Angeles Science Fiction League. There he met professional science fiction writers such as Robert A. Heinlein and Jack Williamson, who became his friends and mentors. They gave him direction and encouragement when he most needed it. He said, "I think these people saved my life in a way."[6]

Success did not arrive overnight for Bradbury. After graduating from high school, he lived at home, working as a newspaper boy. Meanwhile he edited and wrote stories for his own fan magazine, *Futuria Fantasia*, which he started in 1939. He remembers how thrilled he was to be paid $13.75 for his first story, published in 1940. By 1943 he was selling his stories regularly to *Weird Tales*.

The first stories he wrote between age twelve and age twenty-three were semiautobiographical. As a child Bradbury was tormented by fears, nightmares, and scary fantasies. His weird tales of ghosts, vampires, werewolves, and lost souls drew on these memories. *Dark Carnival* (1947), a collection of these stories, "got all of his night-sweats and terrors down on paper."[7] A later story, *Switch on the Night* (1955), was written to calm his own children's fear of the dark. Most of his early stories were published in the science fiction pulps.

In 1947, Bradbury married Marguerite Susan McClure, whom he met in a bookstore. They are still married to each other and have four daughters and eight grandchildren. By then Bradbury had gained recognition as a talented and creative young writer. His rich, poetic style broke away from more simple adventures written at that time. Bradbury's tales fill the reader with wonder at the magic, even horror, that lurks in everyday places.

The Martian Chronicles (1950) and *Fahrenheit 451* (1953) launched Bradbury as a best-selling author. With the extraordinary success of *The Martian Chronicles,* he was able to sell most of his stories to general magazines, no longer needing to depend on pulps. In this way he helped science fiction break into the mainstream. This was important because it introduced many new readers to the work of science fiction writers.

The Martian Chronicles is considered by many to be his greatest work. It is a collection of stories relating how settlers from Earth struggle to colonize

Mars. In the end, an atomic war sends most of the settlers back to Earth. Those left on Mars vow to start a new and better world there. To date, millions of copies have been sold in thirty different languages.

Fahrenheit 451 is set in a future when books are forbidden. Firemen do not put out fires, they set fire to books because the ideas in them could be dangerous. Guy Montag, the hero, changes from a fireman who burns books to a man dedicated to saving them. It is the story of Bradbury himself and his lifelong love affair with books. Today, his books are classics studied in schools and colleges. *Fahrenheit 451* was made into a movie in 1966.

Bradbury returned to the semiautobiographical themes he had explored in *Dark Carnival*, which was republished, with some changes, as *The October Country* in 1955. *Dandelion Wine* (1957) and *Something Wicked This Way Comes* (1962) are based on memories of his Waukegan boyhood. *Dandelion Wine* is set in Green Town, Illinois. The main character, Douglas Spaulding, a twelve-year-old boy, is loosely based on Bradbury himself. The loss of a friend and a new awareness of death move Douglas from childhood toward adulthood. In *Something Wicked This Way Comes*, two fourteen-year-old boys are lured to a traveling carnival that is out to steal their souls.

Many believe that Bradbury wrote his best stories between 1946 and 1955.[8] *The Illustrated Man* (1951) is a collection of some of his best stories. In this collection, fantastic tales are linked by tattoos on the skin of a sideshow freak that come to life.

In the 1960s and 1970s, Bradbury continued to explore fantasy and science fiction themes. These tales, first published in general magazines, were made into collections. For example, *I Sing the Body Electric!* (1969) is about a robot grandmother who helps children feel loved again after their mother dies. Through the years, Bradbury has tried his hand at mystery stories, poetry, drama, film and television scripts, and tales for young readers. *Switch on the Night, The Halloween Tree* (1972), and *Ray Bradbury Presents* (based on his dinosaur tales) were written for young readers. Some of his best-known work has been adapted for movies and television, though not always successfully. He wrote scripts for television adaptations of his work, including *Suspense*, the *Alfred Hitchcock Hour*, and Rod Serling's *Twilight Zone*. Bradbury also hosted and wrote eight episodes for the cable-television series *Ray Bradbury Theater.*

Bradbury has been honored with many awards, including the O. Henry Award for prize stories in 1947 and 1948 and best author for science fiction and fantasy in 1949. He won Academy Award nominations for the animated film *Icarus Montgolfier Wright* (1963). The Science Fiction Writers of America selected him for the Science Fiction Hall of Fame in 1970. At the 1977 World Fantasy Convention, he received a Life Achievement Award. In 1980, he received a Gandalf Award as "Grand

Though he is getting older, Bradbury still remains active in the science fiction world, writing stories and lecturing whenever he gets a chance.

Master" from the WSFS. He also has been honored with the Jules Verne Award (1984). In 1989 he was awarded the Grand Master and Bram Stoker Life Achievement awards. He has never won a Hugo or a Nebula award, perhaps because his writing leans more toward fantasy.

A master storyteller, Bradbury paints magical worlds on Mars, in small midwestern towns, and in dream worlds inside our heads. Bradbury's overlapping worlds challenge us to think about the importance of making good and true choices in our world—for ourselves and mankind. Though his stories have serious themes, his main goal is to entertain and to enchant us.[9] Above all, Bradbury's writing delights the imagination as well as the ear, because he uses vivid language filled with metaphor and rhyme.

Bradbury's critics have said that he is antiscientific because he does not write science fiction about technology. (He is even a little afraid of modern technology. He does not drive a car, he rarely travels by air, and he still uses an old-fashioned typewriter.) Bradbury is not antiscientific. However, he is concerned about the *misuse* of the new powers of science and technology. For example, the danger of human reliance on machinery is illustrated in "The Veldt" (1950), where parents are devoured by "live" lions in the children's futuristic entertainment room. Despite these fears, he still has faith in our ability to use science to shape a better future.[10]

One of the most popular American writers, Bradbury travels around the country, speaking to his fans. Through the power of his imagination, Bradbury has brought alive his "special world, where dreams of tomorrow and memories of yesterday" become fantasies today.[11]

Frank Herbert

Stretching the Powers of the Mind

Frank Herbert was born in Tacoma, Washington, on October 8, 1920, the son of Frank and Eileen Marie (McCarthy) Herbert. Young Frank grew up on the scenic Olympic and Kitsap peninsulas of northwest Washington. His father ran a bus line between Tacoma and Aberdeen and later served on the state highway patrol.

Though his family did not farm, they kept chickens and cows.[1] Frank fished for salmon, hunted for deer, and took homegrown apples to school with his lunch. He felt that living in the country made him "a self-starter" who could think for himself.[2]

Frank's interest in writing and telling stories began early in life. By the age of eight, he wanted to become a writer, he later recalled. By the time he

Frank Herbert

reached his teens, he was telling stories at Boy Scout campfires. His high school English teacher, Homer Post, encouraged him to write for the school newspaper. Around age nineteen, Herbert moved to southern California and got a job with the *Glendale Star*.[3] He worked as a reporter and editor on a number of West Coast newspapers. In 1940 he married Flora Parkinson, but they were divorced in 1945. They had one daughter, Penny.

During World War II, Herbert served in the United States Navy. At the end of the war, he attended school at the University of Washington in Seattle, although he stayed only one year to get training in fiction writing. There he met Beverly Stuart in a short story class.[4] They were married in 1946, and they became the parents of two sons, Brian and Bruce.

His years as a newspaper reporter taught him how to gather accurate information and to write clearly. Herbert's curiosity about new topics grew as he worked on different newspaper stories.[5] In time he taught himself photography, deep-sea diving, and flying. He also studied psychology, religion, and linguistics (languages). He also worked as a professional photographer and television cameraman, a radio news commentator, an oyster diver, a psychologist, and a jungle survival instructor. However, his steadiest work was as a reporter and editor. Later, he used what he had learned and his varied personal experiences to create believable stories.

While working as a reporter, he began publishing science fiction. His first short story, "Looking for Something," appeared in *Startling Stories* in 1952. During the next decade he published about twenty short stories and one novel, *The Dragon of the Sea* (1955). In this novel, Herbert predicted the world-wide oil shortage. This story is set in twenty-first century America, when fuel has to be pirated from the deep undersea wells of an enemy power. A "sub-tug" can tow a giant "slug" containing thousands of barrels of stolen oil. Twenty subs have been destroyed by the enemy. John Ramsey, a psychologist, is assigned duty on the subtug *The Fenian Ram*. Ramsey's mission is to secretly track down a spy on board. *The Dragon of the Sea* foreshadows the powerful writing style of Herbert's Dune novels.

In fact, until the publication of the Dune Trilogy, Herbert was not recognized as a major science fiction writer. Herbert took five years to plan the entire trilogy before he wrote the first book.[6] The trilogy consists of *Dune* (1965), *Dune Messiah* (1969), and *Children of Dune* (1976). The idea for this series began with a magazine article he was writing about the United States Department of Agriculture's control of sand dunes along the Oregon coast. At the time, Herbert was also working on a story about religious cults that take over people's lives. These two subjects, dunes and religion, sparked the idea for what became his masterpiece.[7]

The Dune Trilogy traces the adventures of the Atreides family and is set on the desert planet Arrakis, also known as Dune. Arrakis is the only source in the known universe for melange, a powerful drug. There is a great war to get control of the drug. A young duke, Paul Atreides, becomes the spiritual leader of the native Fremen, who try to save the planet from destruction. Melange comes from giant sandworms. Paul Atreides describes his first glimpse of the giant sandworms of Arrakis:

> Where the dunes began . . . at the foot of a rock beach, a silver-gray curve broached from the desert, sending rivers of sand and dust cascading all around. It lifted higher, resolved into giant, questing mouth. It was a round black hole with edges glistening in the moonlight.
>
> —Herbert, *Dune*

Dune is more than a fairy tale set in the distant future, the twenty-fifth century. It is based on the science of ecology, which is the study of the interaction between living things and their environment. The Dune novels tell the story of the ecological restoration of a desert planet through a violent religious war. Herbert was interested in ecology long before most people had even heard of it.[8] Before writing the Dune books, Herbert spent many years studying ecology, sociology, and religion. His knowledge and understanding of these complex subjects made his imaginary desert world come alive for readers.

In the first novel, Pardot Kynes, a planetologist, discovers that Arrakis was not always a desert world. Vast supplies of water are trapped under the surface. Larvae of the sandworms collect the water to produce melange. When the underground water is released on Arrakis, many unplanned changes come about. Though water makes the planet a fit place for Fremen, it destroys the great worms.

When Arrakis is a desert, the Fremen survive by conserving and recycling every possible trace of moisture, including their own body fluids. They wear stillsuits to recycle their bodies' urine and sweat. After water becomes available, though, they lose their stillsuit discipline. They become "water-fat" and corrupt.

In the Dune Trilogy, Herbert created but then destroyed his heroes. In the first book, Paul is the great spiritual hero who triumphs over his enemies. But Paul falls before his enemies in the second book, *Dune Messiah.* Many science fiction fans were upset by this. But Herbert, the storyteller, wanted his readers to think about the danger of blindly following a leader without asking questions. Although Paul has kept his promise to lead the people to victory, they fall back into the old, bad ways:

> Once . . . long ago he'd thought of himself as an inventor of government. But the invention had fallen into old patterns. It was like some hideous contrivance with a plastic memory. Shape it any way you wanted, but relax for a moment, and it

snapped into ancient forms. Forces at work beyond his reached in human breasts eluded and defied him.

—Herbert, *Dune Messiah*

Herbert wanted his readers to be alert to the dangers of accepting things just the way they are or of returning to old corrupt ways.[9]

Above all, Herbert's forceful writing opens the reader's hyperconscious, stretching the powers of thought and feeling to higher levels. Herbert shows us that exploring and expanding our minds can be a dangerous adventure. To succeed, we must "develop our abilities to the fullest, and meet each crisis as a dangerous opportunity rather than as an occasion for fear."[10]

The Dune works, justly regarded as literary masterpieces, made Herbert rich and famous. *Dune*, the first book of the trilogy, won both a Nebula (1965) and a Hugo (1966). Many believe that *Dune* is the greatest work of science fiction ever written. The first three Dune books have sold millions of copies and have been translated into many languages.

With the commercial success of Dune, Herbert opened the door for many other writers of science fiction. Publishers were willing to increase the amount paid to science fiction writers and even to promote them as best-selling authors. Herbert also made a significant contribution to science fiction. The Dune novels are among the best examples of true scientific imagination. Herbert was not the only science fiction writer to invent awesome new worlds. He was the first, however, to create a novel with an ecological theme based on scientific facts. In *Dune*, Herbert worked out the connection between man and animals, and between geography and climate, so completely that it inspired others to write ecological science fiction.[11]

In 1969, Herbert had become successful enough to stop working as a reporter and editor. He decided to write full-time. Herbert and his wife, Beverly, went to live on a farm in Port Townsend, Washington. He called it an "ecological demonstration project." The purpose of his ecological home was to find alternate sources of energy. It included a heated swimming pool and sauna, a greenhouse for vegetables, solar heating, and a pond for climate regulation. Chickens provided food, fertilizer, and methane gas. Herbert also became involved in computers and windmill design. Around 1980, the family bought a second home on Maui, Hawaii, where they spend half the year.

Herbert wrote over twenty novels, including *The Santaroga Barrier* (1968), *The Dosadi Experiment* (1977), *The Jesus Incident* (1979), and *The Lazarus Effect* (1983). A film was made of *Dune* in 1984. He wrote three sequels to the Dune Trilogy: *God Emperor of Dune* (1981), *Heretics of Dune* (1984), and *Chapterhouse: Dune* (1985).

In the 1970s, Herbert lectured at the University of Washington, Seattle. He also served as a consultant

Herbert gained many fans with his Dune Trilogy and other works.

in social and ecological studies. In 1973 he was director and photographer of a television show, *The Tillers*. From time to time, he attended science fiction conventions. Most of all, though, he seemed to prefer the quiet life on the farm.

In 1984, Herbert's wife of thirty-eight years died of cancer. After returning from the 1986 World Science Fiction Convention in Melbourne, Australia, Herbert learned that he also had cancer. He died while undergoing treatment at the University of Wisconsin in February 1986, at the age of sixty-five. Herbert's work remains a powerful influence in science fiction, inspiring other novelists who share his ecological concerns.

Poul Anderson

Playing the
Science Fiction Orchestra

Poul Anderson was named for his Danish grandfather. His father, Will (Anton) Andersen, changed the family name to Anderson. Will Anderson was born in the United States but was educated in Denmark. He returned to join the Army during World War I. After his discharge from the Army he stayed in America, working as a civil engineer.

Poul's mother, Astrid Hertz, was born in Denmark. She came to America in 1926 to work in the Danish embassy in Washington. While working there, she met Will Anderson, who had attended the same high school in Denmark. They were married soon after. Poul Anderson was born on November 25, 1926, in Bristol, Pennsylvania. When he was less

Poul Anderson

than a year old, the family moved to Port Arthur, Texas. In 1930, his younger brother, John, was born.

They lived in a suburb "full of trees to climb and vacant lots to romp in," Anderson remembers. His father built a boat, and they often went on sailing trips. Poul remembered feeling different from other American boys because of his Danish background: "Our parents took care to keep the family bilingual, another deed for which we remain ever grateful. We celebrated Christmas in the Danish style." They called their mother Mor, which is Danish for Mother. Astrid Anderson took the children along on trips to visit family in Denmark.[1]

When Poul was eleven years old, his father was killed in a car crash. To be with friends and relatives, Mrs. Anderson moved with the boys back to Denmark. Poul said that for him, Denmark felt like another planet. His grandmother was a tall and dignified lady. Cousins of his own age seemed to be more fun than the kids in Texas. But the coming of World War II ended their stay in Denmark. Mrs. Anderson felt that it would not be wise to stay in Denmark with her American sons. They returned to Minnesota in 1939, where Mor bought a forty-acre farm.

"Those years are pretty bad in my memory. I was a social misfit," Poul said later.[2] He had to do farm chores and so could not get in to town. For entertainment he turned to his private world of books. Once while ill, he read science fiction stories from a pile of pulp magazines a friend had sent him. After that he was hooked. He even started writing his own science fiction stories, and he daydreamed about seeing his stories in print one day.

He graduated from high school in 1944 but could not enlist in the Army, because he had damaged eardrums. The University of Minnesota offered an excellent scientific program. Anderson, who planned to become a physicist, decided to go there. Even before he graduated, Anderson began to publish stories.

Over the next fifty years Anderson would produce hundreds of stories. His Danish heritage, particularly Nordic myths, inspired many ideas for his writing. His strong scientific education also shaped the stories he wrote. He said, "Science, technology, history, [myths] the whole world and the universe, provide endlessly fascinating subject matter [for stories]."[3]

In August 1945, atomic bombs were dropped on Hiroshima and Nagasaki, Japan. This historic and terrible event sparked an idea for a story, "Tomorrow's Children," which Anderson wrote with F. N. Waldrop. They sent the story to John Campbell, editor of *Astounding Science Fiction.* Months passed before a letter came from the magazine saying that Campbell would buy the story. "Tomorrow's Children" appeared in *Astounding Science Fiction* in March 1947.

In "Tomorrow's Children," Hugh Drummond finds that Earth has been poisoned by radioactive dust and gases following an atomic war. The radioactivity causes a sharp increase in mutant births, but these sad mutants go on living. At the end of the story, Drummond says that a child born with tentacles instead of arms and legs can "get along all right" if it can learn to use its tentacles. The moral of Anderson's story seems to be that there is hope for the human race, which can survive terrible disasters of its own making. This sad yet hopeful mood, often found in Norse myths, became a trademark of Anderson's work.

Anderson graduated in 1948 with a degree in physics, but he could not find a job in the field. However, he was not too disappointed, because he found that he lacked any special mathematical gift. He began to lose interest in an academic career. In the meantime, he continued to write stories and to sell them to magazines. "Only slowly did it dawn on me that writing had, all along, been what nature cut me out to do," he said.[4]

In 1952 he married Karen Kruse, also a writer. They moved to Berkeley, California, where their daughter, Astrid, was born. Anderson took a job as a chemist at the Department of Agriculture's laboratory, but after nine months he was told that they could not use him. Fortunately, he was beginning to make enough money from writing. In 1953 his writing took off. He published nineteen stories and magazine versions of three novels—*Brain Wave, Three Hearts and Three Lions,* and *War of Two Worlds.*

Brain Wave established Anderson's reputation for excellence. The story tells what happens when Earth moves out from under a galactic cloud covering the solar system. The planet's inhabitants become much more intelligent. Even animals develop memory and intelligence. Mentally challenged humans become normal, while geniuses become capable of superhuman reasoning powers.

In the 1954 winter issue of *Startling Stories,* Anderson published a time chart for a future history, which would become the Technic Civilization series. Anderson borrowed and expanded on this idea from Robert Heinlein. The Technic Civilization series contains two separate sequences. The first sequence centers on Nicholas van Rijn, a merchant prince of the Psychotechnic League, and his interstellar traders. The second sequence begins three hundred years later, during the Terran Empire. The hero, Dominic Flandry, is a tough Terran agent. The Flandry and van Rijn characters highlight Anderson's belief that the best society is one that allows strong, courageous men to survive through freedom of choice. In Technic history, Anderson seems to be offering mankind an escape from repeating the mistakes of the past.[5]

Anderson's Technic Civilization describes the movement of mankind through the universe from A.D. 2100, when man colonizes the Moon and Venus, to A.D. 7100, when a third galactic civilization rises from the ruins of two early civilizations. So far, the series, which makes up a large percentage of Anderson's work, includes about fifty novels.

Anderson's belief in the freedoms and rights of the individual is shown in his Hugo Award-winning short novel, *The Longest Voyage*, published in 1960. The story takes place on a satellite orbiting the giant planet Tambur. Captain Rovic, the hero of the story, and his crew sail their *Viking* ship on a voyage across the seas of the satellite. The ship's crew finds an island ruled by Iskilip, a priest-emperor. Val Nira, an off-worlder whose ship crashed on the island forty years before, is Iskilip's oracle (prophet). Nira needs quicksilver to repair his spaceship and leave, but Captain Rovic does not want Nira to escape. The story ends with the destruction of Nira's spaceship.

The Longest Voyage illustrates why Anderson is known for hard science fiction.[6] He describes in careful detail the temperature, distance, gravity, tides, and rotation of the satellite. He even gives details of the planet's geography, place names, and flora and fauna, including the planet's inhabitants. Anderson stays close to the possible and the probable.

Though Anderson is known for his hard science, he has learned to play all the instruments in the science fiction orchestra, from sword and sorcery to space opera, to future histories and fantasy.

The High Crusade (1960), historical fantasy, shows Anderson's gift for blending history, myth, and

Anderson has touched upon every variation of science fiction and fantasy in his writings.

science. Witty and clever, *The High Crusade* tells the tale of Sir Roger and his band of English knights. The knights defeat a technologically advanced army, using arrows against alien laser guns.

In the 1980s, Anderson continued to write fantasy. The King of Ys series, which he wrote with his wife, Karen, is set in the city of Ys—an ancient Greek and Roman outpost. The story relates how Ys influenced the late Roman Empire.

Anderson's work reflects the changes that have taken place in science fiction writing. In the 1970s, his writing turned toward exploring the deep thoughts and feelings of the characters. For example, in *A Stone in Heaven* (1979), the hero Flandry has changed from the swashbuckling young man in earlier stories. He is aging and graying but much wiser and more thoughtful. Anderson's female characters have changed too. In *The Avatar* (1978), for example, two strong female characters, Joelle and Catlin, help to rescue Dan Broderson from government spaceships that are hunting them down.

Outside of his writing, Anderson says that he is interested in helping the SETI League, an organization of amateur astronomers who search for possible extraterrestrial communication. He also works with the First Millennial Foundation, whose aim is to promote a privately funded space program.[7]

Anderson has received many awards, including five Hugos and two Nebulas, for his short stories and short novels. *The Longest Voyage, No Truce with Kings*

(1964), "The Sharing of Flesh" (1969), *The Queen of Air and Darkness* (1971), and "Goat Song" (1972) all received Hugos. *The Queen of Air and Darkness* and "Goat Song" were awarded Nebulas.

Though Anderson has not produced one great masterpiece, his steady stream of well-crafted stories have been praised as the "backbone of science fiction."[8] His scientific accuracy and in-depth historical research set high standards for science fiction and fantasy writers. Anderson has made an important contribution by highlighting the importance of scientific knowledge without mocking the pleasures of the fantasy world. Anderson believes that "'entertainment' need not be mindless time-killing," like many boring TV sitcoms.[9] He aims to entertain people who enjoy thinking, and according to his thousands of fans, he has done just that.

Andre Norton

Enchanted Worlds

Alice Mary Norton's lifelong love of reading started when she was a very young child. "Books flow in and out of [my life] in an unending stream," she has said.[1] Born February 17, 1912, in Cleveland, Ohio, Alice Mary was a solitary, bookish child. Her mother, Bertha Stemm Norton, read to her often. When she was not reading, she spent hours playing with a collection of miniature animals. Later, her sensitive stories of the animal world reflected this early interest.

Alice Mary's career as a writer began while she was still in high school.[2] She edited the school newspaper, wrote short stories for the literary magazine, and was president of the Quill and Scroll writing society. She attended Western Reserve University

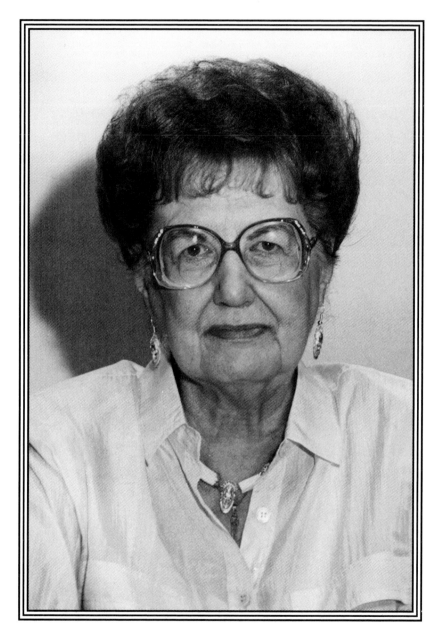

Andre Norton

(now Case Western Reserve University) from 1931 to 1932, planning a career as a history teacher. Her plans were interrupted by the Great Depression, and she had to quit college.

After leaving college, Norton became a children's librarian in the Cleveland Public Library. Around that time she began writing and publishing historical fiction for young readers. In her early twenties, she sold *The Prince Commands* (1934), under the name Andre Norton. In 1938 she wrote *Ralestone Luck*, another historical adventure. With the publication of these books, Norton legally changed her name from Alice Mary to Andre because male writers sold more easily at that time.

For the library's story hours, she wrote and read legends and tales to the children. This inspired her to write her own stories. Norton wrote four adventure stories for young adults. *Follow the Drum* (1942) is the story of the settlement of Maryland. *Scarface* (1948) tells the tale of a pirate in the West Indies. *Yankee Privateer* (1955) concerns a marine during the Revolution. *Stand to Horse* (1956) is set during the Apache wars of the late 1850s. "All of these required long months of research and delving into old records, volumes of letters, Army reports, and much revision," she said.[3]

During World War II, Norton worked as a special librarian for a citizenship project in Washington, D.C., and as a librarian at the Library of Congress. At this time she began reading letters from the people of the Netherlands, who were resisting the Nazis. These letters gave her the idea for three spy novels set in that country: *The Sword Is Drawn* (1944), *Sword in Sheath* (1949), and *At Swords' Point* (1954). The Netherlands government awarded her a special plaque for her understanding of their struggles.

After twenty years as a librarian, Norton left to work as a reader at Gnome Press in 1951. For a few years she even tried her hand at managing a bookstore. All along she kept writing and publishing. In 1958, she quit her other jobs to become a full-time writer.

In the early 1950s, Norton switched from historical novels to science fiction. Having read and collected science fiction for her pleasure, she decided to write her own stories. Her first attempt, *Star Man's Son* published in 1952, developed into a series of Star stories. *Star Man's Son* was followed by *Star Rangers* (1953), *Star Guard* (1955), and *Star Gate* (1958). From then on, Norton wrote science fiction novels at the rate of two to three a year.

In *Star Man's Son*, Norton skillfully relates the coming of age of young Fors, a mutant. Fors runs away to prove himself a Star Man, or explorer. Along with Arskane, a black youth who befriends him, Fors is successful in uniting several clans against the Beast Things. Many consider the author's first science fiction novel to be one of her best.

In *Star Gate*, as in many of her tales, Norton's belief that people need to learn to accept and respect all living things comes through clearly. The hero of *Star Gate*, Kincars'Rud, forms a bond with a mord (a cross between a vulture and a bat) and a larng (a four-eyed, hairy steed). The mord and larng help him in his adventures.

The Star novels are fast-paced space operas. In these tales Norton does not give detailed descriptions of technology, as many other science fiction writers do. Yet, few writers are better at inventing things and giving names to them. In her novels, spaceships seem as ordinary as buses. Flitters transport things, stunners and blasters deal with enemies, coms of all kinds keep people in touch, and countless other imaginary devices perform many functions.[4]

In the 1960s, Norton began to focus on writing series. The Witch World series, begun in the early 1960s, became Norton's masterpiece. Norton based this series on her research into the Crusades of the Middle Ages.

Witch World (1963)—which starts when Simon Tregazrth passes through a stone entryway (the Siege Perilous) and finds himself in the land of Estarp on the planet Witch World—is more fantasy than science fiction. On this alien planet, magic is more powerful than technology. The power of magic rests with the Council of Witches, whose spiritual powers are stronger than men's steel weapons. In *Witch World* and other tales, Norton often uses objects rather than machines as sources of power. Their power can be used only by those with special gifts.

Jewels of power are important in the Witch World series.

With the great success of the Witch World series, Norton went on to produce several other series. These include the Magic series, the Dane Thorson or Solar Queen series, the Ross Murdock series, the Holsteen Storm series, and the Janus series.

Norton began her Magic series in the mid-1960s. These fantasies for young people include *Steel Magic* (1965) and *Octagon Magic* (1967). Those written in the 1970s include *Dragon Magic* (1972) and *Red Hart Magic* (1976). In *Dragon Magic*, the main characters are two troubled young people. Sig Dortmund is a slow learner, while George "Ras" Brown is torn between his father's patriotism and his brother's militant support of black power. In *Red Hart Magic*, Chris Fitton and Nan Mallory are upset at being away from their parents for a long time. In the Magic series, as in the Witch World series, objects can produce magic.

Norton describes herself as an old-fashioned storyteller with morals.[5] For example, her westerns have strong heroes and evil villains. Her heroes and heroines are American Indians, mutants, aliens, or troubled young people. Often they are misfits who must suffer many ordeals to reach self-understanding. Their quests end in bonding with other beings: human, alien, or animal. Norton emphasizes the freedom and honor of the individual. Her characters are not superhuman, as Frank Herbert's are in

Though she has won many awards and is respected throughout the science fiction community, Norton remains a private person and rarely makes public appearances.

Children of Dune and *God Emperor of Dune.* They are real to the reader because they have weaknesses just as the reader does.

Norton is a private person who does not give many interviews or attend public meetings. Because of poor health, she moved from the Midwest to Florida. In her home she has a miniature animal collection, a huge library, and a number of cats to keep her company.

Norton considers the completion of the Witch World series and the Senses series to be her most significant work in the last five years. Outside of her writing Norton says her plan for a writer's colony in Tennessee (called High Hallack, after an imaginary world in one of her series) is most significant to her. In 1997, Norton moved from Florida to Tennessee to begin establishing a retreat, reference, and research library. When completed, the library will be open to those writing various types of fiction, both juvenile and adult, and those writing about science fiction.[6]

Norton deserves praise for the unusual variety of her work: fantasy, science fiction, romance, historical fiction, murder mysteries, and poetry. Norton's work is a colorful blend of different types of fiction, set in worlds of the past, the future, parallel universes, or on distant planets.

Norton has received credit for shaping a new point of view for science fiction and fantasy writers: Scientific knowledge alone cannot save mankind from destruction. She helps readers to understand spiritual power to solve their problems and fulfill their needs. Many writers have made use of Norton's point of view, including Ursula K. Le Guin.

By portraying powerful women, Norton has made an important contribution to science fiction. The third book of her Witch World series, *Year of the Unicorn* (1965), broke with the science fiction and fantasy tradition of portraying strong, violent male heroes. Indeed, Norton is the first fantasy writer to tell stories from a more feminine point of view—a point of view that focuses on the need to avoid violence and to have men and women work together to solve problems.[7]

Many honors have been bestowed on Norton. Among them are a Hugo Award nomination in 1962; the Gandalf Master Fantasy Award for lifetime achievement in 1977; and the Grand Master Award for Science Fiction in 1984. She was the first woman to receive that award. These are proper recognition for a writer who has made important contributions to science fiction and fantasy and continues to entertain and awe her readers.

Madeleine L'Engle

Madeleine L'Engle
Mystical Storyteller

Madeleine L'Engle Camp was born in New York City on November 29, 1918. Her parents, Madeleine (Bennett) Camp, a talented pianist, and Charles Wadsworth Camp, a writer, led busy lives. They often went out to dinners, plays, and concerts. Madeleine remembered her parents' apartment filled with artists of one kind or another.[1]

As an only child of busy parents, Madeleine spent many hours alone, and she developed a love of reading and writing stories for her own amusement. Young Madeleine did not even mind eating supper alone in her room. There she could let her imagination run free with wonderful ideas for stories. "She wrote her first story at age five and began to keep a personal journal at age eight;" thus began her lifelong habit of writing about her daily experiences.[2]

Madeleine was not happy at the first elementary school she attended. She was the last to be chosen for teams because she was not athletic. Too shy to make friends, and called dumb by her teachers, she felt very unpopular. To add to her sense of unhappiness, Madeleine lived in constant fear that her father might die. His lungs had been badly burned by mustard gas during World War I. She had nightmares that there would be another terrible world war.[3]

To escape from sadness and ease her fears, Madeleine wrote fantasy stories in which her wishes could come true.[4] Today she still writes out of personal need. She says that her stories spring "from the writer's need to understand life."[5]

Madeleine did not show her writing to her teachers, but she did enter one of her poems in a school contest. When her poem won first prize, her teacher accused her of copying it. To prove that her daughter had not cheated, Madeleine's mother showed other stories and poems to the teacher. After that her parents decided to send Madeleine to private school in New York City. There, Madeleine's sixth-grade teacher encouraged her to develop her writing talent.

When Madeleine was twelve, her father became seriously ill with pneumonia. After he was well enough to travel, the family moved to Europe "searching for places where Father could breathe more easily."[6] They spent the first summer in a large, old château in the French Alps. Madeleine was happy there because she had time to daydream. "I wandered through the centuries, being the daughter of the château, Madeleine in the twelfth century, the fifteenth, the eighteenth. I wrote stories and poems," she said.[7]

This dream world ended when her parents sent her off to boarding school in Switzerland. "It was, at first, sheer hell," she said.[8] The school was bitterly cold in the winter, and the food tasted bad. Worst of all, Madeleine had no time to write or daydream. She cried herself to sleep each night. Through her tears she could see Lake Geneva and the snow-covered mountains of France, and she began to make up stories about the mountains. Bedtime became the most important time of day, for then she could let her imagination run free.

When she turned fourteen, the family returned to the United States to take care of her grandmother. Madeleine enjoyed the summer at her grandmother's beach house in Florida. At summer's end, her parents sent her to Ashley Hall Boarding School in Charleston, South Carolina. This time she settled into life at the boarding school more easily. At Ashley she was popular with her peers. In her senior year she edited the school magazine.

Then followed four years at Smith College in Northampton, Massachusetts. She said, "I did a great deal of growing up, and a lot of this growing was extremely painful. I cut far too many classes, wrote dozens of short stories, and managed to get an excellent education despite myself."[9]

After graduating from Smith College in 1941, L'Engle returned to New York to become a writer. To support herself, she took small parts in plays. Several of L'Engle's short stories were published in magazines. In 1945, her first book, *The Small Rain*, was published. Many autobiographical details, especially difficulties she faced while growing up, are reflected in this book.

Katherine Forrester, the main character of *The Small Rain*, is a talented pianist whose first teacher was her mother, a famous musician. Katherine went to boarding school in Switzerland and was a lonely and unhappy teenager, just as Madeleine had been. On Katherine's return to New York City, she finds that her social life and engagement to a young actor are interfering with her music studies. In *The Small Rain*, Katherine's mother dies. Madeleine's father had died shortly before she wrote the novel.

At play rehearsals, L'Engle met and fell in love with Hugh Franklin, a handsome young actor. They were married in 1946. Their first child, Josephine, was born a year later. The Franklins decided to move to the country to get away from the tensions of city life. They had bought a two-hundred-year-old farmhouse, Crosswicks, in Connecticut. To make a living they ran a small general store. In 1952, their second child, Bion, was born. And in 1957, they also adopted a girl, Maria, who was the orphaned daughter of their best friends.

These were difficult and busy times for L'Engle and her growing family. She worked in the store, ran the farmhouse, and raised her three children. Somehow, though, she still made time to write at night. She said, "My love for my family and my need to write were in acute conflict. The problem was that I put two things first. My husband and children came first. So did my writing."[10]

Despite all her efforts, she only had one book published between 1950 and 1959. On her fortieth birthday she got another rejection letter. She burst into tears and decided to stop wasting her time writing. She covered up her typewriter and walked around the room crying. A moment later some ideas popped into her head. She uncovered the typewriter and got back to work.[11] In her memoir, *A Circle of Quiet* (1971), L'Engle recalled thinking, "If I never had another book published, and it was very clear to me that this was a real possibility, I still had to go on writing."[12]

After seven years at Crosswicks, the family decided to move back to New York City. Hugh, her husband, returned to his acting career. He became famous as Doctor Charles Tyler on the television serial *All My Children*. L'Engle taught writing in the high school at St. Hilda's and St. Hugh's Anglican School. In her leisure time she attended plays, art exhibits, and met other writers. All these things helped to fire her imagination.

At this time L'Engle began *Meet the Austins* (1960), the story of a spoiled young orphan who comes to live with the close-knit, loving Austin family. Vicky Austin, a spunky sixteen year old, is the main character. The book was named an American Library Association Book of the Year, and it launched a popular series of juvenile fiction. Other titles in the Austin series include *The Moon by Night* (1963) and *The Twenty-Four Days Before Christmas* (1964).

The first Austin book prepared L'Engle for what was to become her masterpiece, *A Wrinkle in Time*. Just before the move to the city, the Franklins went on a ten-week camping trip across the United States. On the trip, the idea for *A Wrinkle in Time* began to form. Madeleine completed the book soon after the trip. After being rejected twenty-six times in two years, it was finally published in 1962.

Early one morning L'Engle got a telephone call. *A Wrinkle in Time* had won the Newbery Medal. She was so happy she rushed into the bedroom and leaped on the bed to tell Hugh the great news. After writing for nearly three decades, she had won the most notable prize in children's literature. *A Wrinkle in Time* is the first science fiction novel for young readers to receive such special honors.[13] The book went on to become a classic, and it made many fans for Madeleine L'Engle. After that she no longer had to worry about her writing being rejected.

A Wrinkle in Time is both science fiction and fantasy. It portrays three supernatural creatures, Mrs. Who, Mrs. Whatsit, and Mrs. Which, so it includes elements of fantasy. The novel also describes a futuristic mode of space travel and speculates about the possibility of life in the universe, so it includes elements of science fiction. The book relates the adventures of Meg Murry, Charles Wallace Murry, and their friend Calvin O'Keefe, who must save the world from doom. Guided by the three supernatural creatures, they travel through space and time in a desperate effort to rescue Mr. Murry, who vanishes while exploring the existence of the tesseract, a means of "wrinkling" time and space. They find Mr. Murry on planet Camazotz, where the inhabitants have been brainwashed and act like robots.

The children are faced with many difficult decisions and struggle to choose good over evil. Young readers can easily understand Meg and Calvin, who like other teens are concerned about their physical appearance, their parents' problems, and peer and sibling rivalries. Meg, a lively and independent female heroine, was a welcome change from the weak female characters often portrayed in science fiction literature at that time.

To base her story about time travel on scientific fact, L'Engle read the theories of physicists Albert Einstein and Max Planck. After *A Wrinkle in Time,* she wrote the follow-ups *A Wind in the Door* (1973) and *A Swiftly Tilting Planet* (1978). She called these three novels the Time Trilogy, since each book is about the Murry family and time travel. *A Swiftly Tilting Planet* considers how history might be changed if a person could travel backward in time. Like *A Wrinkle in Time*, it remains a favorite with L'Engle's readers.

In the 1970s, L'Engle began writing nonfiction, starting with *A Circle of Quiet.* This became the first of three volumes of memoirs based on her Crosswicks Journals. From them, readers learn directly of her life and hopes. In 1972, when her ninety-year-old mother died, L'Engle recorded this sad event in *The Summer of the Great-Grandmother* (1974). Soon after, L'Engle feared that she might go blind from the eye diseases iritis and glaucoma. Though her illness caused her great pain, she continued to give lectures and to inspire young writers.

In the 1980s, the Franklins traveled to Egypt and China as cultural representatives of the United States. Shortly after they returned, Hugh was diagnosed with cancer. He died four months later. L'Engle felt deep pain at the loss of her husband after forty years of happy marriage. She wrote *Two-Part Invention* (1988) to tell the story of their life together.

Biblical themes have become especially important to L'Engle. In the novel *Certain Women* (1992), for example, the character of David Wheaton parallels the story of the biblical David. Her husband's

Despite health problems, L'Engle keeps a busy schedule and continues to lecture all over the country.

illness also shaped Wheaton, a dying retired actor who must make peace with his family.

Over the years she has also been writer-in-residence at several colleges, including Wheaton College in Illinois, to which she donated a collection of her papers. For her achievements, she has received many honorary degrees from both American colleges and theological seminaries. She was the recipient of the 1998 Margaret A. Edwards Award, honoring her lifetime contribution to writing for teens. Though now in a wheelchair, L'Engle continues to write and give lectures and readings.

Although best known as a children's writer, L'Engle never talks down to her young readers. Instead, she says, when an idea becomes too difficult for grownups, then she presents it to young people.[14] L'Engle, the mystical storyteller, has been justly praised for a special ability to blend scientific principles with the quest for higher meaning, and she has been praised for her skillful development of believable characters who deal with modern-day problems in both realistic and fantastic settings.[15]

Ursula K. Le Guin

Fantastic Anthropologist

The youngest of four children, and the only girl in the family, Ursula Kroeber Le Guin was born October 21, 1929, in Berkeley, California. Her father, Alfred Kroeber, was a professor of anthropology, and her mother, Theodora, was a writer. From an early age Ursula's parents' interests and careers stimulated her writing. Professor Kroeber wrote books about the Indians of California. His friendship with Ishi, a California Indian, became the subject of Theodora Kroeber's classic book, *Ishi in Two Worlds: A Biography of the Last Wild Indian in North America* (1961). As a child, Ursula enjoyed hearing her father retelling Indian legends.

The Kroebers' interest in studying different cultures inspired Ursula to create imaginary cultures of

Ursula K. Le Guin

her own. Le Guin would later set her stories in four invented worlds: Earthsea, the Hainish planets, Orsinia, and a future American West Coast. "My father studied real cultures and I make them up—in a way, it's the same thing," she said.[1] Ursula also loved to read, especially myths, fairy tales, and science fiction in *Amazing Stories*.[2] Around her twelfth birthday she read a grown-up book set in a world of fantasy. For the first time, she realized that adults were still making up new myths.

During the school year, the family lived near the University of California campus in Berkeley, where her father taught. Their summer home was an old, tumbledown ranch in the Napa Valley, sixty miles north of San Francisco. It was also a gathering place for scientists, writers, students, and California Indians. Ursula heard a lot of interesting grown-up conversation, which sparked her thinking and imagination.

When Ursula was eleven years old, she submitted one of her science fiction stories to *Amazing Stories*. It was rejected.[3] She vividly remembers her brother Karl sitting on the stairs looking up at her and saying, "I'm afraid this is your story come back." Ursula was not really downcast, though. Instead, she felt flattered by receiving a real rejection slip like an adult.[4]

After graduating from Berkeley High School, she chose to go east to college. At Radcliffe and Columbia, in New York, she studied French and

Italian Renaissance poetry. She received a scholarship in 1952 to continue her studies in France. On the way over aboard the *Queen Mary* she met Charles Le Guin. They had a shipboard romance and were married in Paris on Christmas Day 1953.[5]

To stay with her husband, who was a professor, Le Guin quit work on her doctoral degree. She instead went to work as a secretary at Emory University in Atlanta, Georgia, in 1953. She then worked as a part-time instructor in French at Mercer University in Macon, Georgia, in 1954 and at the University of Idaho in Moscow in 1956. In 1959, the Le Guins settled in Portland, Oregon, where Charles Le Guin taught history at Portland State University. In the years following, Le Guin raised three children, Elisabeth, Caroline, and Theodore. At night, she made time for her writing.

During the 1950s, Le Guin wrote five novels, four of them set in the imaginary European country of Orsinia. But she could not get them published. In the 1960s, she began writing science fiction and fantasy to try to get her stories into print. She sold her first stories about time travel to *Fantastic Stories* and *Imagination* magazines. Le Guin says it took time to develop her full powers as a writer: "She calls her first published novels 'fairy tales decked out in space suits.'"[6]

These beginning science fiction stories became part of the Hainish Cycle, a series of tales in which all humans originate from a common ancestor on the planet Hain. In these novels, the humanoid race settles on eighty-four planets in the galaxy, including Earth. After a galactic war, settlers on the different planets lose contact with one another. Long after the war, the Hainish begin to communicate with one another again. The Hainish heroes visit distant planets and find similar beings among alien populations. After many struggles, they finally come to understand that these aliens are humans like themselves.

Le Guin's Hainish stories received much praise. Though set on imaginary planets, they explore important subjects that lead readers to think about the need to respect others. They also start readers thinking about the need to build a perfect society (or utopia) by making honorable choices right here and now.[7]

The three most important Hainish novels are *The Left Hand of Darkness* (1969), *The Word for World Is Forest* (1976), and *The Dispossessed* (1974). These three novels won the Hugo Awards. *The Left Hand of Darkness* and *The Dispossessed* also won Nebula Awards.

In the late 1960s, Le Guin was asked by Parnassus Press to write a novel for young adults. The theme of islands and magic had sparked her imagination in earlier stories. This led her to write *A Wizard of Earthsea,* her first book for young readers published in 1968. She wrote *The Tombs of Atuan* in 1971 and *The Farthest Shore* a year later. *Tehanu: The Last Book of Earthsea* was published in 1990.

These novels are set in the fantasy world of Earthsea, made up of many islands set in a vast crystal-clear sea. Readers follow the adventures of Ged, who must make the difficult journey from childhood to adulthood. Guided by wise men, Ged learns to control his magic, to balance good and evil, and to keep the fragile balance or equilibrium between the earth, the sea, and its people. Earthsea has been highly praised for its strong, thoughtful themes, vivid worlds, and colorful characters. Earthsea is considered to be among the most influential of all twentieth-century fantasy writing.[8]

After the fantasy world of Earthsea, and the science fiction Hainish world, Le Guin turned to Orsinia. The Orsinian stories are historical fiction. Orsinia is a fictional country located in Europe in the distant and near past of Western civilization. Le Guin refers to historic events that actually took place in these tales. "I was in college when I started the pieces that eventually became the *Orsinian* tales. . . . I made up a place that was like the places in books I liked to read. . . . I [made] up just enough of the rules to free my imagination."[9] *Orsinian Tales,* a collection of short stories, was published in 1976. It received a nomination for the National Book Award in 1977. Le Guin published an Orsinian novel, *Malafrena,* in 1979. Other Orsinian short stories appeared in *The New Yorker* magazine in the 1980s.

The Orsinian tales do not follow a chronological order (from past to present), but they share common ideas, themes, and images. The Orsinian books are moral fables set in an alternate earth similar to our own. Through these tales, Le Guin helps readers see that though evil lurks in the world, heroic actions can win the day. "The Road East," for example, tells the story of a young man, Maler Eray, who must choose between loyalty to his mother and commitment to his fellow Orsinians, who are risking their lives in a revolution.

The setting for Le Guin's fourth world is the American West Coast in the twenty-first century. After disasters, pollution, wars, earthquakes, and volcanic eruptions, people try to rebuild a better world. In *The Lathe of Heaven* (1971), George Orr has special powers to change reality through his dreams. Dr. Haber, a government psychiatrist, tricks Orr into using his dreams to change the world in horrible ways. A television movie of *The Lathe of Heaven* was made in 1980. In the American West novels, Le Guin continues thought experiments on ways to create a perfect world or utopia and on ways to overcome our present-day problems. In building these worlds, Le Guin uses the same methods that her father used to study Native American culture. She describes them in great detail as if she lived there, even creating maps for her readers to follow. The reader sees them as very real. Yet the reader also comes to understand that all these strange worlds are really images of Earth.[10]

Though she keeps very busy, Le Guin likes to relax at home.

Ursula K. Le Guin is considered one of the most important and most elegant science fiction and fantasy writers today. She draws her ideas from many different sources, including myths, legends, poetry, history, and Chinese philosophy. Her stories are an unusual blend of romance, fantasy, mythology, philosophy, science fiction, and historical fiction.

Le Guin's characters are searching for a balance between opposites. This theme of opposites springs from her discovery of the *Tao Te Ching* of Lao Tzu, the Chinese philosopher. Using this metaphor of opposites, Le Guin is able to create rich and beautiful language that sounds like poetry. In *The Tombs of Atuan,* for example, Tenar, the young priestess, struggles to balance the powers of good and evil, and light and darkness. And she learns that

> The Earth is beautiful, and bright, and kindly, but that is not all. The Earth is also terrible, and dark, and cruel. The rabbit shrieks dying in the green meadows. The mountains clench their great hands full of hidden fire.
>
> —Le Guin, *The Tombs of Atuan*

Le Guin has been invited to teach writing workshops on university campuses, and she is an active member of writers' associations. In the 1960s, she spoke out against the Vietnam War and worked in the presidential campaigns of Democratic candidates who opposed that war.

In the 1990s, she has published three collections of stories: *A Fisherman of the Inland Sea* (1994), *Four*

Ways to Forgiveness (1995), and *Unlocking the Air* (1996). She also wrote a volume of poetry, an English version of Lao Tzu's *Tao Te Ching* (1997), and a children's book, *Wonderful Alexander and the Catwings* (1994). Outside of writing, her most recent significant event was a trip to Tierra del Fuego on the tip of South America.[11]

Among the many honors she has received are the Newbery Medal for *The Tombs of Atuan*. *The Farthest Shore* won the National Book Award for Children's Literature. For her novels and stories, she has been honored with Nebula, Hugo, and Gandalf awards.

Le Guin insists that science fiction and fantasy writing "is to be judged, not as schlock, not as junk."[12] Indeed, Le Guin has set high standards for fantasy and science fiction writers to follow.

Octavia E. Butler

Breaking Down Barriers

Octavia Estelle Butler started writing her own stories when she was about twelve years old. "When I was 12, I was watching a bad science fiction movie (*Devil Girl From Mars*), and I decided that I could write a better story than that. And I turned off the TV and proceeded to try, and I've been writing science fiction ever since." That story grew into her first published novel, *Patternmaster* (1976).[1]

Octavia Butler, born June 22, 1947, is the first African-American woman to gain fame as a science fiction writer. Her father, Laurice Butler, died when she was still a baby. She was brought up by her mother and grandmother in a poor neighborhood of Pasadena, California.

Octavia E. Butler

Octavia did not feel singled out as a young black girl, because a mix of African-American, Asian, Asian-American, Hispanic, and white people lived in her neighborhood.[2] However, she did notice that her mother, who worked as a maid, was not always treated with respect by those she worked for. Butler recalled, "I used to see her going to back doors, being talked about while standing right there . . . being treated like a nonperson."[3]

Her grandmother told her stories about growing up on a Louisiana sugar plantation. From her mother and grandmother, then, Octavia began to understand that life had been hard for her ancestors. Many years later, Octavia wrote *Kindred* (1979), the frightening story of Dana, an African-American woman. Dana suddenly finds herself transported back to the nineteenth-century South to save the life of a white boy, Rufus Weylin. Rufus turns out to be a distant ancestor, and so the bond of family ties them to each other. In this novel, and in many of her later novels, Butler shows the importance of the family. Butler says that she wrote *Kindred* to make others feel the pain and fear that black people lived through in order to survive.[4]

An only child, Octavia spent most of her time alone, reading and daydreaming. She was too shy to make friends or take part in school or church activities. Giving oral reports in class terrified her. This shyness and fear of speaking in public made her seem slow and unintelligent.

In junior high school, Octavia found teachers who understood her problems. Miss Peters, her seventh-grade home economics teacher, took time to read her stories and to encourage her. Mr. Pfaff, her eighth-grade science teacher, stimulated a love of science. He even corrected and typed the first story she ever submitted to a science fiction magazine.[5]

Butler's mother wanted her to continue her education after her graduation from John Muir High School in 1965, but Butler was afraid of going to college. She started by working during the day and taking classes at night.[6] She graduated from Pasadena City College in 1968 with a two-year degree. After that she attended California State University, Los Angeles. After a year, though, she quit because there were too few courses in creative writing.[7] In *Kindred,* Butler describes the jobs she took to support herself at the time. Dana, Butler's black heroine, says:

> I was working out of a casual labor agency—we regulars called it a slave market. . . . You swept floors, stuffed envelopes, took inventory, washed dishes, sorted potato chips (really!), cleaned toilets. . . . You did whatever you were sent out to do. . . . I did the work, I went home, I ate, and then slept for a few hours. [Then] I got up and . . . [got] busy working on my novel.[8]

Butler believes that the most valuable help she received with her writing was from two workshops she attended.[9] The first was the Open Door Program of the Screen Writers' Guild of America, West. The second was the Clarion Science Fiction Writers' Workshop. Harlan Ellison, a well-known science fiction writer, taught some of the classes and liked Butler's writing. One of her short stories was published in the Clarion anthology. Though Butler kept on writing and sending in her stories, she could not get them published. Friends and family told her to get a "real job." But after five years, her first book was published. *Patternmaster* sold well enough for Butler to become a full-time writer.

Butler is best known for her novels set in the world of Patternists, which cover hundreds of years of human history. The Patternist books— *Patternmaster, Mind of My Mind* (1977), *Survivor* (1978), *Wild Seed* (1980), and *Clay's Ark* (1984)— are about a society of telepaths. These telepaths want to create a race of superhumans. Doro, the four-thousand-year-old immortal who founded the society, survives by taking over the bodies of young humans. The novels relate the struggle to stop Doro and his telepaths from carrying out their evil plans.

The heroines of Butler's books are strong black women who learn to understand and love those who are trying to attack them. In *Wild Seed*, for example, Doro selects Anyanwu, the "wild-seed" shape-changer, to breed a race of superior humans with him. But Doro's plans are blocked by Anyanwu, who is immortal and does not need to kill to survive. Mary Larkin, Doro's light-skinned daughter, is the strong heroine portrayed in *Mind of My Mind.* Mary struggles to break free of Doro's control. To put an end to his murderous rule, she organizes the telepaths against Doro.

In *Survivor,* Butler also explores the issue of race. *Survivor's* heroine, Alanna, is an Afro-Asian woman who is taken to another planet to escape a virulent disease that is killing earthlings. On this alien planet, the most important leaders are able to change their color to blue. Alanna, like many of Butler's heroines, helps to break down the barriers between men and women of different races.

Parable of the Sower (1993), Butler's tenth novel, centers on an eighteen-year-old woman who tries to heal a world that no longer cares about suffering. Butler's heroine is one of the most resourceful young African-American women in print.[10] She invents ways to survive in a world destroyed by hate and fear and to face the future with love and courage. Butler says that in American society today, though people fear crime and violence, it does not have to be that way.[11]

In 1985, Butler won top honors for best novelette, the Nebula Award, and the Hugo Award for "Bloodchild," the horrifying story of the love between a human boy, Gan, and an alien woman, T'Gatoi.

"Bloodchild" is set on a planet where human males can bear the children of aliens by hatching eggs inserted into them. Butler says that she was trying to

Butler's science fiction novels deal with many social issues affecting our own society.

do something different with the "invasion story." Most novels about humans colonizing other planets have followed two patterns.

> Either the aliens resist and humans have to conquer them violently, or they submit and become good servants. I don't like either of those alternatives, and I wanted to create a new one. I mean science fiction is supposed to be about exploring new ideas and possibilities. In the case of "Bloodchild," I was creating an alien that was different from us, though still recognizable—a centipede-like creature. But you're not supposed to regard it as evil.[12]

In 1995, Butler received a MacArthur Foundation Fellowship. MacArthur Foundation winners are chosen on the basis of their skill, creativity, and dedication. As well as the honor, she received a $295,000 grant to continue writing. She has been rightly recognized for creating black heroines and for exploring the issue of race in a new setting. In doing this, Butler has overturned some of the old science fiction traditions that centered around white male heroes. However, Butler's contribution to science fiction does not come from favoritism toward blacks or women. Instead, she emphasizes the urgent need to break down all race and gender barriers. Butler's tales seem to tell her readers to unite with one another to bring out what is best in them.

Butler says that she is a fifty-year-old writer who can remember being a ten-year-old writer and who expects someday to be an eighty-year-old writer. She describes herself as a hermit living in a city; a student, endlessly curious; a feminist; an African American; a former Baptist; and an oil-and-water combination of ambition, laziness, insecurity, certainty, and drive.[13] Following her interests wherever they lead, questioning and learning as she goes, is a great pleasure for Butler. Writing has given her the freedom to earn a living exploring the many things that fascinate her. "I love words, their sounds, their multiple meanings and shadings, the power we give them to teach and to wound, to build and to heal."[14]

Chapter Notes

Introduction

1. Frederik Pohl, "The Study of Science Fiction: A Modest Proposal," *Science-Fiction Studies*, vol. 24, 1997, pp. 11–16.

2. John Clute and Peter Nicholls, eds., *The Encyclopedia of Science Fiction* (New York: St. Martin's Griffin, 1995), p. 409.

3. Ann Evory and Linda Metzger, eds., *Contemporary Authors*, New Revision Series, vol. 11 (Detroit: Gale Research, 1984), p. 410.

Chapter 1. Robert A. Heinlein: Shaking the Reader Loose

1. Laurie Collier and Joyce Nakamura, eds., *Major Authors and Illustrators for Children and Young Adults*, vol. 3 (Detroit: Gale Research, 1988), p. 1093.

2. H. Bruce Franklin, *Robert A. Heinlein: America as Science Fiction* (New York: Oxford University Press, 1980), p. 7.

3. Collier and Nakamura, p. 1093.

4. Franklin, p. 12.

5. Ibid., p. 13.

6. Ibid.

7. Ibid., p. 14.

8. Everett F. Bleiler, ed., *Science Fiction Writers* (New York: Charles Scribner's Sons, 1982), p. 188.

9. John Clute and Peter Nicholls, eds., *The Encyclopedia of Science Fiction* (New York: St. Martin's Griffin, 1995), p. 555.

10. John J. Pierce, *Foundations of Science Fiction* (New York: Greenwood Press, 1987), p. 185.

11. Jeff Chapman, Pamela S. Dear, and John D. Jorgenson, eds., *Contemporary Authors*, New Revision Series, vol. 53 (Detroit: Gale Research, 1997), p. 240.

12. Collier and Nakamura, p. 1095.

13. Robert A. Heinlein, *Grumbles from the Grave*, ed. Virginia A. Heinlein (New York: Ballantine, 1989), p. 43.

14. Heinlein, p. 245.

Chapter 2. Isaac Asimov: Astonishing, Astounding, and Amazing

1. James E. Gunn, *Isaac Asimov: The Foundations of Science Fiction* (New York: Oxford University Press, 1982), p. 7.

2. Isaac Asimov, *Isaac Asimov: A Memoir* (New York: Doubleday, 1992), p. 43.

3. Ibid., p. 45.

4. Ibid., p. 30.

5. Ibid., p. 70.

6. Gunn, p. 13.

7. Asimov, p. 121.

8. Gunn, p. 9.

9. Asimov, p. 109.

10. Ibid., p. 151.

11. Ibid., p. 62.

12. Gunn, p. 10.

13. Asimov, p. 153.

14. John Clute, ed., *Science Fiction: The Illustrated Encyclopedia* (New York: Dorling Kindersley, 1995), p. 135.

15. Thomas M. Disch, "Quantum Leap," *Entertainment Weekly*, April 17, 1992, p. 53.

16. Asimov, p. 334.

Chapter 3. Frederik Pohl: Master of Buying, Selling, and Writing Science Fiction

1. Frederik Pohl, *The Way the Future Was: A Memoir* (New York: Ballantine Books, 1978), p. 8.

2. Ibid., p. 9.

3. Ibid., p. 31.

4. Alexei and Cory Panshin, *The World Beyond the Hill: Science Fiction and the Quest for Transcendence* (Los Angeles: Jeremy P. Tarcher, 1989), p. 257.

5. Ibid., p. 81.

6. Anne Commire, ed., *Something About the Author*, vol. 24 (Detroit: Gale Research, 1981), p. 165.

7. Pohl, p. 179.

8. Commire, p. 166.

9. Frederik Pohl, personal correspondence with author, October 30, 1997.

10. Ibid.

11. Commire, p. 166.

Chapter 4. Ray Bradbury: Dreaming the Past-Future

1. Ray Bradbury, *The Stories of Ray Bradbury* (New York: Alfred A. Knopf, 1980), p. xiv.

2. Wayne L. Johnson, *Ray Bradbury* (New York: Frederick Ungar, 1980), p. 1.

3. James Lesniak, ed., *Contemporary Authors*, New Revision Series, vol. 30 (Detroit: Gale Research, 1990), p. 41.

4. David Mogen, *Ray Bradbury* (Boston: Twayne, 1986), p. 4.

5. Ibid., p. 5.

6. Ibid., p. 7.

7. "Bradbury, Ray," *Current Biography*, vol. 43, July 1982, p. 3.

8. John Clute, ed., *The Encyclopedia of Fantasy* (New York: St. Martin's Press, 1997), p. 133.

9. Bryan Ryan, ed., *Major 20th-Century Writers*, vol. 1 (Detroit: Gale Research, 1990), p. 365.

10. Mogen, p. 21.

11. Johnson, p. 146.

Chapter 5. Frank Herbert: Stretching the Powers of the Mind

1. Timothy O'Reilly, *Frank Herbert* (New York: Frederick Ungar, 1981), pp. 14–15.

2. Ibid., p. 15.

3. William F. Touponce, *Frank Herbert* (Boston: Twayne, 1988), p. 5.

4. Ibid.

5. Everett F. Bleiler, ed., *Science Fiction Writers* (New York: Charles Scribner's Sons, 1982), p. 377.

6. Frank N. Magill, *Surveys of Science Fiction Literature*, vol. 2 (Englewood Cliffs, N.J.: Salem Press, 1979), p. 647.

7. Ibid.

8. Bleiler, p. 378.

9. O'Reilly, p. 151.

10. Magill, p. 652.

11. Susan M. Trotsky, ed., *Contemporary Authors*, New Revisions Series, vol. 43 (Detroit: Gale Research, 1994), p. 202.

Chapter 6. Poul Anderson: Playing the Science Fiction Orchestra

1. Agnes Garrett and Helga P. McCue, eds., *Authors and Artists for Young Adults*, vol. 5 (Detroit: Gale Research, 1990), p. 6.

2. Ibid.

3. Everett F. Bleiler, ed., *Science Fiction Writers* (New York: Charles Scribner's Sons, 1982), p. 9.

4. Garrett and McCue, p. 4.

5. John J. Pierce, *Foundations of Science Fiction* (New York: Greenwood Press, 1987), p. 216.

6. Bleiler, p. 259.

7. Poul Anderson, personal correspondence with author, August 8, 1997.

8. Marilyn P. Fletcher, ed., *Reader's Guide to Twentieth-Century Science Fiction* (Chicago: American Library Association, 1989), p. 2.

9. Garrett and McCue, p. 12.

Chapter 7. Andre Norton: Enchanted Worlds

1. Roger C. Schlobin, "Andre Norton: Humanity Amid the Hardware," in *The Feminine Eye: Science Fiction and the Women Who Write It*, ed. Tom Staicar (New York: Frederick Ungar, 1982), p. 26.

2. Muriel Fuller, ed., *More About Junior Authors* (New York: H. W. Wilson, 1963), p. 159.

3. Ibid., p. 159.

4. Roger Elwood, ed., *The Many Worlds of Andre Norton* (Radnor, Pa.: Chilton Book Company, 1974), p. vii.

5. Charlotte Spivak, *Merlin's Daughters: Contemporary Women Writers of Fantasy* (New York: Greenwood Press, 1987), p. 23.

6. *Cyclopedia of World Authors*, 3rd ed., vol. 4 (Englewood Cliffs, N.J.: Salem Press, 1997), p. 1504.

7. Andre Norton, personal correspondence with author, October 30, 1997.

Chapter 8. Madeleine L'Engle: Mystical Storyteller

1. Muriel Fuller, ed., *More About Junior Authors* (New York: H. W. Wilson, 1963), p. 137.

2. Carole F. Chase, *Madeleine L'Engle, Suncatcher* (San Diego: LuraMedia, 1988), p. 22.

3. Madeleine L'Engle, *The Summer of the Great-Grandmother* (New York: Seabury Press, 1979), p. 113.

4. Ibid., p. 140.

5. Chase, p. 33.

6. L'Engle, p. 95.

7. Ibid., p. 96.

8. Ibid., p. 98.

9. Ibid., p. 132.

10. "L'Engle, Madeleine," *Current Biography*, vol. 58, January 1997, p. 35.

11. Doreen Gonzales, *Madeleine L'Engle: Author of* A Wrinkle in Time (New York: Dillon Press, 1991), p. 75.

12. Madeleine L'Engle, *A Circle of Quiet* (New York: Farrar, Strauss, and Giroux, 1971).

13. Laura Standley Berger, ed., *Twentieth-Century Children's Writers*, 4th ed. (Detroit: St. James Press, 1995), p. 564.

14. "L'Engle, Madeleine," p. 35.

15. Karen Funk Blocher, *The Tesseract, A Madeleine L'Engle Bibliography in 5 Dimensions,* 1997, <http://members.aol.com/kfbofpql/Lengl.html> (June 11, 1998).

Chapter 9. Ursula K. Le Guin: Fantastic Anthropologist

1. Elizabeth Cummins, *Understanding Ursula K. Le Guin* (Columbia: University of South Carolina Press, 1990), p. 2.

2. Laurie Collier and Joyce Nakamura, eds., *Major Authors and Illustrators for Children and Young Adults,* vol. 4 (Detroit: Gale Research, 1992), pp. 1434–1435.

3. "Le Guin, Ursula K.," *Current Biography,* January 1983, p. 24.

4. Ursula K. Le Guin, *The Language of the Night* (New York: G. P. Putnam's Sons, 1979), p. 26.

5. "Le Guin, Ursula K.," p. 25.

6. Collier and Nakamura, p. 1434.

7. Ursula K. Le Guin, *A Fisherman of the Inland Sea* (New York: HarperPrism, 1994), p. 5.

8. John Clute and Peter Nicholls, eds. *The Encyclopedia of Science Fiction* (New York: St. Martin's Griffin, 1995), p. 704.

9. Cummins, pp. 128–129.

10. Susan Wood, "Discovering Worlds: The Fiction of Ursula K. Le Guin," in *Voices for the Future,* vol. 2, ed. Thomas Clareson (Bowling Green University Popular Press, 1979), p. 154.

11. Ursula K. Le Guin, personal correspondence with author, September 12, 1997.

12. Ursula K. Le Guin, *The Language of the Night,* p. 127.

Chapter 10. Octavia E. Butler: Breaking Down Barriers

1. L. Mpho Mabunda, ed., *Contemporary Black Biography,* vol. 8 (Detroit: Gale Research, 1995), p. 38.

2. Jessie C. Smith, ed., *Notable Black American Women* (Detroit: Gale Research, 1991), p. 144.

3. Mabunda, p. 38.

4. Ibid., p. 39.

5. Smith, p. 145.

6. Ibid.

7. *African American Biography*, vol. 1 (Detroit: Gale Research, 1994), p. 110.

8. Octavia, Butler, *Kindred* (Boston: Beacon Press, 1988), pp. 52–53.

9. Octavia E. Butler, personal correspondence with author, August 9, 1997.

10. Pearl Cleage, "Summer Reading," *American Visions,* vol. 9, June/July 1994, p. 30.

11. Stephen W. Potts, "'We Keep Playing the Same Record': A Conversation with Octavia E. Butler," *Science-Fiction Studies*, vol. 23, November 1996, p. 334.

12. Ibid., p. 332.

13. Octavia E. Butler, personal correspondence with the author.

14. "Finding Our Voice," *Essence*, vol. 26, May 1995, p. 193.

Further Reading

Asimov, Isaac. *Science Fiction, Science Fact.* New York: Dell Publishing Co., 1991.

———. *Space Spotter's Guide.* New York: Dell Publishing Co., 1991.

Bloom, Harold, ed. *Science Fiction Writers of the Golden Age.* New York: Chelsea House, 1995.

Clute, John, and Peter Nicholls. *The Encyclopedia of Science Fiction.* New York: Saint Martin's Press, 1995.

Freas, Frank K. *A Separate Star.* West Hills, Calif.: Kelly Freas Studios, 1984.

Hartwell, David G., ed. *Science Fiction Century.* New York: Saint Martin's Press, 1997.

James, Edward. *Science Fiction in the Twentieth Century.* New York: Oxford University Press, 1994.

Judson, Karen. *Isaac Asimov: Master of Science Fiction.* Springfield, N.J.: Enslow Publishers, 1998.

London, Brooks. *Science Fiction after 1900.* New York: Macmillan Library Reference, 1997.

MacNee, Marie J. *Science Fiction, Fantasy, & Horror Writers.* 2 vols. Detroit: Gale Research, 1994.

Magill, Frank N. *Science Fiction Alien Encounter.* Johnstown, Pa.: Salem Press, 1986.

Peel, John. *The Invaders.* New York: Tor Books, 1998.

Simon, Seymour. *Space Monsters: From Movies, TV and Books.* New York: HarperCollins Children's Books, 1977.

Stover, Leon E. *Robert A. Heinlein.* Boston: Twayne, 1987.

Sullivan, C. W. III, ed. *Science Fiction for Young Readers.* New York: Greenwood Publishing Group, 1993.

Tuck, Donald H. *Encyclopedia of Science Fiction & Fantasy.* 3 vols. New York: Advent Publishers, 1983.

Internet Addresses

Analog Science Fiction and Fact
<http://www.sfsite.com/analog>
Publishes on-line stories and provides science facts.

Fantasy and Science Fiction Magazine
<http://www.fsfmag.com>
Publishes on-line articles and new science and fantasy fiction stories. Contains links to many other resources.

Science Fiction, Fantasy, and Horror Book Database
<http://books.ratatosk.org/>
Contains biographies and bibliographies of authors, links to home pages of authors, and resources for purchasing books.

Selected Bibliography

Robert A. Heinlein

Stranger in a Strange Land. New York: Putnam, 1961.
The Past Through Tomorrow: "Future History" Stories. New York: Putnam, 1967.
I Will Fear No Evil. New York: Putnam, 1970.
Time Enough For Love, or The Lives of Lazarus Long. New York: Putnam, 1973.
Starship Troopers. London: New English Library, 1975.

Isaac Asimov

I, Robot. Garden City, N.Y.: Doubleday, 1950.
The Intelligent Man's Guide to Science. New York: BasicBooks, 1960.
Constantinople: The Forgotten Empire. Boston: Houghton Mifflin, 1970.
The Collapsing Universe. London: Hutchison, 1977.
Extraterrestrial Civilizations. New York: Crown Publishers, 1979.
Foundation's Edge. South Yarmouth, Mass.: J. Curley, 1982.

Frederik Pohl

and C. M. Kornbluth. *The Space Merchants.* New York: Walker, 1953.
Gateway. New York: St. Martin's Press, 1977.
Beyond the Blue Event Horizon. New York: Ballantine Books, 1980.
The Other End of Time. New York: Tor Books, 1996.

Ray Bradbury

The Illustrated Man. Garden City, N.Y.: Doubleday, 1951.

Fahrenheit 451. New York: Ballantine Books, 1953.

The Martian Chronicles. Garden City, N.Y.: Doubleday, 1958.

Something Wicked This Way Comes. New York: Simon and Schuster, 1962.

Frank Herbert

Dune. Philadelphia: Chilton Books, 1965.

Dune Messiah. New York: Putnam, 1969.

The God Makers. New York: Putnam, 1972.

The Dosadi Experiment. New York: Putnam, 1977.

Poul Anderson

Brain Wave. New York: Walker, 1954.

The Queen of Air and Darkness. Boston: Gregg Press, 1973.

The Day of Their Return. Garden City, N.Y.: Doubleday, 1973.

A Knight of Ghosts and Shadows. Garden City, N.Y.: Doubleday, 1974.

Andre Norton

The Sword Is Drawn. Cambridge, Mass.: Houghton Mifflin, 1944.

Star Man's Son, 2250 A.D. New York: Harcourt, Brace, 1952.

Star Gate. New York: Harcourt, Brace, 1958.

The X Factor. New York: Harcourt, Brace and World, 1965.

Madeleine L'Engle

A Wrinkle in Time. New York: Ariel Books, 1962.

The Summer of the Great-Grandmother. New York: Farrar, Straus, and Giroux, 1974.

A Ring of Endless Light. New York: Farrar, Straus, and Giroux, 1980.

and Maria Rooney. *Mothers & Daughters.* Harold Shaw Publishers, 1997.

Ursula K. Le Guin

A Wizard of Earthsea. Berkeley, Calif.: Parnassus Press, 1968.

The Lathe of Heaven. New York: Scribner, 1971.

The Word for World Is Forest. New York: Berkley Publishing Corp., 1972.

Orsinian Tales. New York: Harper and Row, 1976.

Octavia E. Butler

Patternmaster. Garden City, N.Y.: Doubleday, 1976.

Wild Seed. Garden City, N.Y.: Doubleday, 1980.

Clay's Ark. New York: St. Martin's, 1984.

Parable of the Sower. New York: Four Walls Eight Windows, 1993.

Index